SIGN LANGUAGE FLASH CARDS

VOLUME I
THIRD EDITION

SIGN LANGUAGE FLASH CARDS
VOLUME I
THIRD EDITION

by

Harry W. Hoemann, Ph.D.
Department of Psychology
Bowling Green State University

and

Shirley A. Hoemann, M.F.A.
1435 Rosewood Drive
Bowling Green, OH 43402

Published by the Bowling Green Press, Inc.
        P.O. Box 582
        1435 Rosewood Drive
        Bowling Green, Ohio 43402

ISBN #0-9614621-5-9 (Previously ISBN #0-913072-10-9)

INDEX

This index was prepared so that instructors could locate signs that they wished to assign to students and so that students could find ASL equivalents of English words. The items that appear in all caps are the glosses that apply to the illustrations on the cards. Items that appear in lower case are related signs that are described on the cards. Lower case references are generally omitted from the index if an illustrated reference is available.

A

ABANDON 276
ABBREVIATE 338
ABILITY 72
ABOUT 39
ABOVE 15
ACCEPT 218
accident 325
accompany 476
ACOUSTICALLY DEAF 460
ACROSS 209
ACT 122
actor 419
add 38
address 446
adult female 244
adult male 244
advance 202
advertise 153
ADVISE 53
advisor 53
AFRAID 255
AFRAID 48
AFTER 209
AFTER WHILE 262
AFTERNOON 402
afterward 30
AGAIN 352
against the law 287
against the rules 372
age in years 110
AGENT 18
AGO 118
agree 452
AIRPLANE 1
ALL 494
all afternoon 228, 402
all along 174
all day 250
all four of them 395
ALL GONE 393
all morning 228
ALL RIGHT 302
all three of them 395
ALONE 179
ALREADY 214
ALSO 452
ALWAYS 370
AMERICA 485
AMONG 451
AND 46
angel 490
ANGRY 144

ANGRY 384
anniversary 457
announce 378
ANOTHER 348
ANSWER 378
ANY 75
anyone 75
anything 75, 268
ANYWAY 169
appear 411
APPLE 264
APPLY 131
apply for a job 427
approach 163
archery 406
area 44
ARGUE 273
ARGUE 97
army 290, 421
AROUND 433
ARRANGE 79
ARRIVE 221
ashamed 283
ASK 436
assist 495
assistant 495
ASSOCIATE 185
ATTEMPT 149
ATTRACTED TO 80
AUTUMN 299
AVENGE 479
avoid 184
awaken 32, 207
AWFUL 296
AWKWARD 455

B

BABY 478
back up 375
BAD 492
bank a plane 1
banquet 491
bake 339
BARE 294
basketball 406
BE ABLE 72
BE ATTRACTED TO 80
be careful 304
be quiet 454
BEAR (noun) 379
BEAUTIFUL 152
BECAUSE 318

BECOME 28
BEER 345
beer 17
BEFORE 30
BEGIN 124
BEHAVE 122
BELIEVE 203
below 15
best 270
better 270, 342
BETWEEN 331
Bible 303
BIG 473
BIRD 111
BIRTH 135
birthday 135
bitter 162, 475
BLACK 284
BLAME 396
blame myself 396
blank mind 120
blind 381
BLOOD 195
BLUE 353
blush 425
board 106
boast 480
BOOK 237
boring 67
BORROW 311
BOTH 395
bother 331
BOUND 279
boxing 406
BOY 238
brag 480
BRAVE 382
BREAD 56
BREAK 233
brief 361
BRIGHT 462
BRING 91
BROKE 350
brother 238, 452
BROWN 17
BUG 113
BUGGY 113
BUILD 159
BUILDING 159
burn 317
business 86
busy 122
BUT 164
buy 7, 447

C

California	387
CALL	29
call on a phone	257
CAN	72
CANDIDATE	131
candle	317
CANDY	92
CAN'T	372
CAR	375
careful	304
CARELESS	453
CARELESSLY	453
CARRY	91
CAT	371
CATHOLIC	103
celebrate	457
CENT	417
CENTER	449
chain	33
chair	206
CHAIRPERSON	254
CHANGE	484
chapter	85
character	468
CHARGE	36
chase	184
CHEESE	477
chef	339
chemist	31
CHEMISTRY	31
chicken	111
CHIEF	270
CHIEFLY	270
CHOKED UP	230
choked up with anger	230
choked up with laughter	230
CHOOSE	271
Christ	4
Christian	303
chronically ill	20
CHURCH	213
city	154
class	421
CLEAN	112
clean house	112
clean up	112
cleaner	270
CLEAR	462
CLEVER	443
climb stairs	293
climb with a plane	1
clomp	293
close	52
close friend	314
close the window	259
CLOTHES	313
COFFEE	128
COLD	272
COLLEGE	127
COME	204
come near	163
COMFORT	49
COMFORTABLE	49
command	151, 383
commandment	287
commandments	287
COMPARE	363
COMPLAIN	300

complete	470
completed	470
CONCEAL	100
CONDENSE	338
CONFESS	487
CONFESSION	487
confessional	487
CONFUSED	325
CONGRESS	107
CONSCIENCE	468
CONSERVE	172
consume	491
CONTINUE	278
CONTRACTIONS	281
CONTROL	409
CONVERSATION	151
CONVERSE	151
cook (noun)	339
COOK (verb)	339
COOKIE	43
COOL	189
cooperate	33
COP	374
copy	47
COPY ME	47
CORRECT	68
COST	36
COUNSEL	53
counselor	53
COUNT	461
COUNTRY	401
COUNTRYSIDE	401
COURT	306
COUSIN	220
covet	354
COW	219
crash a plane	1
crippled	455
CROSS (adj.)	144
cross (verb)	209
CRUEL	139
culturally deaf	460
CUP	54
CURIOUSITY	37
CURIOUS	37
CUTE	92

D

daily	104
dance	188
DARK	438
daughter	51, 478, 500
DAY	250
DEAF	460
deaf	460
DEATH	241
debt	126
deceive	362
DECIDE	147
deep blue	353
deer	200, 219
DEFEAT	355
DEFEND	177
delicious	416
DEPART	98
DEPEND	133
depressed	493
DESERTED	294

DESPISE	466
deteriorate	472
DEVIL	490
DIE	241
DIFFERENT	164
DIFFICULT	426
dime	417
DIRT	65
DIRTY	3
disagree	45
DISAPPEAR	481
DISAPPEAR	411
DISAPPOINT	475
DISAPPOINTED	475
disciple	184
discontinue work	193
DISCUSS	97
DISSOLVE	481
DIVIDE	399
division	399
DO	122
do stunts	1
DOCTOR	93
DOLLAR	319
DONATE	474
DONE	214
DON'T	50
DON'T CARE	102
DON'T CARE	169
don't do that	372
DON'T KNOW	434
don't like	434
DON'T WANT	282
DOUBT	337
doubt	337
downtown	449
draftsman	316
DRAMA	419
draw	359
DREAM	181
drill press	105
driving rain	9
drop	193
DROP OUT	411
drop out of sight	481
drunk	345
DRY	67
duck	111
DUMB	389
during	174
duty	86

E

EACH	158
EACH OTHER	185
eagle	111
EAR	224
EARTH	358
earthquake	358
east	161
EASY	428
EAT	491
eat it all up	491
EGG	71
ELECT	59
ELECTRIC	89
ELECTRICITY	89
elephant	200

embarrassed	425	fencing	406	gentleman	22, 238
EMPHASIZE	431	FEW	496	GET	445
EMPTY	294	fifty cents	417	get even	73
END	470	FIGHT	273	giraffe	200
enemy	45, 273	FIGURE	132	girl	40, 500
engineer	316	fill out forms	427	GIVE	474
enjoy	42, 310	FINALLY	288	GIVE UP	274
ENOUGH	121	FIND	258	glass	54
ENSLAVED	279	FINE (verb)	36	GO	312
enter	242	FINE (adj.)	444	go across	209
ENVY	354	FINGERSPELL	418	go in	242
EQUAL	73	FINGERSPELLING	418	go out	242
escape	411	FINISH	214	go through	168
establish	136	FINISH	470	go with	476
eternity	370	FIRE	317	GOD	170
EVEN	73	FIRE FROM A JOB	397	GOLD	387
evening	228, 402	fireman	374	gone	241
every	158	FIRST	116	GOOD	342
every day	104	FIRST OF ALL	116	good friend	314
every monday	328	FISH	323	GOVERNMENT	256
every month	482	fishing	406	governor	256
every week	326	FIT	119	GRADUATE	407
every year	349, 497	five cents	417	grandfather	341
everything	268	fix	210	GRANDMOTHER	341
EVIDENCE	377	flashlight	462	grasping	448
EXACT	68	flee	411	grass	364
EXAGGERATE	153	FLOWER	125	GRAVY	439
EXCEED	101	flunk	285	greedy	448
exceeding	101	fly a plane	1	green	353
EXCEPT	330	FOLLOW	184	grief	196, 289
EXCEPTIONAL	330	follower	184	GROUND	65
EXCESS	101	food	491	GROUP	421
EXCHANGE	117	fool	138	GROW	364
exchange gifts	474	FOOLISH	138	GUARD	177
EXCITED	493	FOOTBALL	406	guess	175
EXCUSE	386	FOR	404	GUILT	468
EXCUSE ME	386	for a duration of time	174	
EXPECT	12	FOR SOME TIME	346	
expensive	81, 447	force	355	H
EXPERIENCE	373	foresee	150	
EXPERT	69	forever	370	HAPPEN	174
		FORGET	120	HAPPY	310
		FORGIVE	386	HARD	367
F		FORK	173	HARD	426
		foundation	495	hard of hearing	460
FACTORY	105	four cents	417	HARM	391
FAIL	285	four weeks ago	10	HATE	466
fail an exam	285	four weeks from now	10	HAVE	292
FAIR	73	fourth	116	HE	192, 403
fake	362	fourthly	116	headache	344
fall (verb)	188	FOX	483	headlights	462
FALL (noun)	299	FREE	467	HEALTHY	382
FALSE	440	FREEZE	365	HEAR	224
FALSE	362	freshman	336	hearing person	383
family	421	Friday	322, 329	HEART	289
FAMOUS	394	FRIEND	314	HEAVEN	186
FANCY	444	frog	37	HELP	495
FAR	340	FROM	16	helpless	260
FAR AWAY	340	FULL	225	her	307, 410, 469
FARM	129	FUN	229	her	192, 403
farmer	129	FUNNY	376	herd	421
FAT	83	FUTURE	360	HERE	142
favorite	416			hers	307, 410
FEAR	255			herself	87
FEAR	48	G		HIDE	100
feast	491			him	192, 403
feeble-minded	315	GALLAUDET	463	himself	87
feed	491	GALLAUDET UNIVERSITY	463	his	307, 410, 469
FEEL	442	garage	375	HOME	489
FEMALE	500	generous amount	101	HONOR	334

HOPE 12
horse 219
HOSPITAL 201
HOT 441
HOT 498
hot to the touch 498
HOUR 422
HOUSE 154
HOW? 178
how many? 34
how much? 34
HUH? 183
HUMBLE 368
HUNGRY 165
hunting 406
HURRY 88
hurt 13
HUSBAND 245

I

I 192
ICE CREAM 109
IDEA 134
IGNORANT 236
IGNORE 70
ill at ease 455
illegal 287
imagine 134, 181
IMITATE MY SIGNS 47
IMPORTANT 343
impossible 372
IMPRESS 431
IMPROVE 472
IN 242
in back of 30
in excess of 101
in front of 30
INDIFFERENT 169
insect 113
INSIDE 242
INSTEAD OF 117
INSTITUTION 136
INTELLIGENT 239
INTELLIGENT 443
INTERESTED 388
INTERESTING 388
INTERPRET 90
interpreter 90
INTRODUCE 261
investigate 82
invite 29
it 192, 403
Italy 103
itch 113
its 307, 410, 469
itself 87

J

JEALOUS 354
JESUS 303
JEW 222
JEWISH 222
JOIN 33
JUDGE 306

jump 188
Junior 336

K

KEEP 304
KEEP PUTTING OFF 308
KEY 95
KILL 450
killer 450
KIND 6
KINDNESS 6
KING 4
kitchen 339
kneel 188
KNOW 14

L

LADY 22
lag behind 184
LAID OFF 160
land a plane 1
language 216, 263
large 473
LAST 288
LAST WEEK 10
last year 349, 497
LATE 166
late afternoon 228, 402
LATER 360
LATER 262
LAW 287
lawyer 18
LAY OFF 160
LAZY 182
LEAD 146
lead astray 146
leader 146
LEARN 217
LEAVE 276
LEAVE 98
lecture 156
left 161
legislature 107
lend 311
LEVEL 73
LIE 440
lie down 188
LIFE 446
LIGHT 462
light sprinkle 9
LIKE 80
LIKE 42
limit 101
limited 101
lipread 465
LIST 85
LISTEN 224
little boy 244
little girl 244
LIVE 446
living room 444
loaf 167, 182
LOCK 95
long ago 118
LONG FOR 165
LONG TIME 297

LOOK 413
look around 381, 413
look at 381
look at me 381, 413
look back 381, 413
LOOK FOR 41
look forward 381
Lord 4
LOSE 408
LOUSY 398
LOVE 366

M

MACHINE 105
MAGIC 488
MAKE 210
make a copy 47
make a list 85
make a request 436
makes no difference 169
MALE 238
MAN 238
MANY 34
MARRY 248
MAYBE 19
ME 192
me too 452
MEAN 139
MEAN 144
MEASURE 316
MEAT 64
MEDICINE 11
MEET 235
MEET 223
MEETING 235
MELT 481
MEMORIZE 335
mercy 148
MESH 119
MIDDLE 449
MILK 265
MINE 307
mingle 185
MINUTE 424
MISS 175
MIXED 325
MONDAY 328
MONEY 447
MONKEY 55
MONTH 482
monthly 482
moon 456
MORALLY RIGHT 302
MORE 38
MORNING 228
MOST 301
MOTION PICTURE 61
MOVE 286
move away 286
MOVIE 61
much 473
mule 77, 219
MULISH 77
MULTIPLY 132
MUSIC 332
MUST 62
MY 307
MYSELF 87

N

NAKED 294
NAME 385
narrow 473
NATION 194
natural 194
naturally 194
NEAR 163
near future 360
NEED 62
neighbor 163
nephew 220
NEVER 390
NEVERTHELESS 169
NEW 212
NEXT 202
next week 10, 326
NEXT YEAR 497
NICE 112
niece 220
night 228
NO (verb) 380
NO (adj.) 50
none 50
NONE OF MY BUSINESS 155
NOON 228, 402
north 161
NOT 249
NOT RESPONSIBLE 155
NOT YET 298
NOTHING 392
notice 82, 359
NOW 2
NUMBER 305
NUMERAL 305
nurse 93

O

OBEY 414
OBTAIN 445
ocean 405
O'CLOCK 187
ODD 5
often 352
OK 302
OLD 110
on either side 30
on Mondays 328
on the left side 30
on that side 30
ON THE CONTRARY 164
on the right side 30
on this side 30
ONCE 471
once in a while 471
one 471
ONE ANOTHER 185
one year 349
ONLY 179
OPEN 52
open the window 259
OPPOSED 45
OPPOSITE 45
OR 333
order 151
OTHER 348
OUGHT 62

OUR 410
ours 307, 469
ourselves 87
out 242
OUT OF MONEY 350
OVER 15
OVERCOME 355
owe 126

P

PAIN 344
pale faced 459
PAPER 464
paragraph 85
parking lot 375
participate 211
party 26
pass 184
PAST 118
PATH 143
PATIENT (adj.) 13
patient (noun) 201
PAY 126
PEACE 454
PECULIAR 5
peddler 78
peeved 384
PEOPLE 320
PEPPER 267
perfect 68
PERHAPS 19
PERSON 18
personality 468
perspire 195
perverse 302
PHEW! 81
philosophy 21
photocopy 47
PHYSICIAN 93
physics 89
PICK 271
pick on 479
PICTURE 115
pig 3
pink 425
PITY 148
PLACE 44
PLAN 79
PLAY (verb) 26
PLAY (noun) 419
PLEASANT 189
PLEASE 42
pleasure 42, 289, 310
poetry 332
poison 11
POLICEMAN 374
POLITE 444
pool 406
POOR 324
pop up 411
POSSESS 292
postpone 308
POTATO 329
POUNDS 215
PRACTICE 191
PRAISE 57
PRAY 436

PREACH 156
preacher 156
predict 413
prefer 416
pregnant 260
Preparatory 336
PREPARE 79
prepared 275
PRESENT 2
PRESIDENT 254
PREVIOUSLY 30
PRICE 36
PRIDE 480
prince 4
princess 4
PRINCIPAL 35
principle 287
print 359
prisoner 18
problem 426
PROCRASTINATE 308
progress 202
PROLONG 153
PROMISE 198
PROOF 377
prophesy 413
prostitute 283
PROTESTANT 197
PROUD 480
PROVE 377
publicity 153
publicize 153
pull over 375
PUNISH 74
PUNISHMENT 74
pure 112
purple 353
PURPOSE 404

Q

QUARREL 273
quarter 417
queen 4
quick 361
quiet 454
QUIT 211

R

RAILROAD 25
RAIN 9
rarely 471
READ 208
READY 275
REALLY 291
REBEL 58
RECEIVE 445
recently 118
RED 425
red faced 425
refuse 58
REGISTER 427
regularly 68
REIGN 409
religion 468

REMAIN 278
remote future 360
repair 210
repeatedly ill 20
research 82
RESIDENTIAL SCHOOL 136
respect 334
RESPONSIBILITY 400
RESPONSIBLE 400
rest room 176
REVENGE 479
rich 7, 447
RIGHT (side) 161
RIGHT (morally) 302
RIGHT (correct) 68
river 143
ROAD 143
ROCK 232
roommate 119
RUIN 139
RULE 409
RUN 23
run away 411
run into a ditch 375

S

SAD 106
SALT 295
SAME 452
satan 490
SATISFIED 190
Saturday 322, 329
SAVE 172
SAVE 467
Savior 279, 467
SAW 141
SAY 383
SCHOOL 277
SCIENCE 31
scientist 31
SEARCH 41
second 116
SECOND 424
secondly 116
SECRET 420
SEE 381
SEEK 41
SELECT 271
self pity 148
sell 78
SENIOR 336
sensitive 442
sentence 216
separate 33
servant 91
several 496
shame on you 283
share 399
she 192, 403
SHEEP 327
shiny 387, 458
SHIP 231
SHOES 253
shop 7, 447
SHORT 40
SHORT TIME 361
SHOULD 62

SHOW 247
shun 466
shut 52
SHY 283
SICK 20
SIGN 263
sign forms 427
SIGN YOUR NAME 427
SILLY 138
silver 387
similar 452
SIN 309
SINCE 346
SING 332
sister 452, 500
SIT 206
six cents 417
skepticism 337
SKILLED 69
skunk 200
sky 186
slacks 313
SLEEP 32
SLOW 114
SLOWLY 114
small 244
small amount 101
SMART 443
SMART 239
SMELL 27
snore 141
snow 9
socialize 185
SOFT 266
SOIL 65
SOLDIER 290
SOME 60
something 60, 268
sometimes 471
SON 51
SONG 332
soon 360
Sophomore 336
SORROW 196
SORRY 196
sort 6
SOUP 109
SOUR 162
south 161
speak 269
SPECIAL 330
SPEECH 465
SPEECHREAD 465
SPOIL 391
SPOON 347
SPRING 364
STAND 188
STAR 108
stare 381, 413
START 124
start a car 95
STAY 278
STEAL 130
still 278
stink 27
stockings 313
stomach ache 344
STOMACH CRAMPS 281
stomp 293
STOP 430

STORE 78
STORY 216
stove 317
STRANGE 5
stream 143, 412
STREET 412
strict 367, 426
strive 199
STRONG 382
struggle 45, 199
STUBBORN 77
STUCK 260
student 18, 217
STUDY 82
STUPID 389
SUBTRACT 415
SUCCEED 486
SUCCESS 486
suffer 13
SUGAR 92
SUMMARIZE 338
SUMMER 441
SUMMON 29
sun 456
SUNDAY 322
SUNSHINE 456
SUPERINTENDENT 254
supervise 304
supervisor 304
SURE 291
SURPRISE 207
SURPRISED 207
suspend 133
suspicion 337
swallow 66
SWEAR 198
sweat 195
SWEETHEART 84
SWEET 92
swimming 406

T

table saw 105
take 445
take a picture 115
take off 1
TAKE UP 193
TALL 244
TARDY 166
TASTE 416
tavern 345
TAX 36
TEA 157
TEACH 123
teacher 18, 123
team 421
TEASE 391
TELEPHONE 257
tell 383
tell a story 216
temple 213
TEMPT 429
TEMPTATION 429
ten cents 417
tennis 406
tent 154
TERRIBLE 296
THAN 94

THANK 246
THANK YOU 246
THANKS 246
THAT 351
their 307, 410, 469
theirs 307, 410, 469
them 192, 403
themselves 87
these 351
they 192, 403
thin 83
THING 268
THINGS 268
THINK 226
third 116
thirdly 116
THIRSTY 66
THIS 351
this month 2
this morning 2
this week 2
this year 2
those 351
THOUGHT 226
three cents 417
three hours 422
three times 471
three weeks 326
three weeks ago 10, 326
three weeks from now 10
three years 349
three years from now 497
thrilled 493
THROUGH 168
Thursday 322, 329
tickle 113
TIGER 200
TIME 187
TIME 234
times 187
tiny 473
TIRED 63
TO 240
toast 173
today 2
TOILET 176
TOMORROW 104
tonight 2
TOO 452
TOO MUCH 101
TOUCH 458
touchy 442
TOWARD 240
town 154
TRADE 117
TRAIN 25
TREE 150
trinity 395
triune 395
trousers 313
TRUE 291
TRULY 291
trust 203
TRY 149
Tuesday 322, 329
turn a corner 375
twice 471
two cents 417
two hours 422
two months 482

two weeks 326
two weeks ago 10, 326
two weeks from now 10
two years 349
two years ago 349, 497
two years from now ... 349, 497

U

UGLY 171
UNCLE 280
uncomfortable 300
UNDER 251
UNDERSTAND 24
UNDERTAKE 193
United States 485
university 127, 463
UNTIL 145
UNTIL NOW 346
upright 302
US 432
USE 205
USE UP 393
USED UP 393

V

VACATION 167
vague 438
VALUE 343
VARIETY 96
VARIOUS 96
vary 96
vehicle 231
very 473
very dry 67
very fond 366
very ill 20
very intelligent 81
very late 166
very slow 114
very slowly 114
VICTORY 457
vinegar 437
VISIT 227
VOICE 269
VOLUNTEER 131
VOTE 59

W

WAIT 435
waiter 95
waitress 95
WALK 293
walk aimlessly 293
walk laboriously 293
walk slowly 293
walk uphill 293
WANT 448
WAR 199
WARM 356
warn 29
WASH CLOTHES 99
washing machine 99
WASTE 7
watch 413

WATER 405
WAY 412
way too much 101
WE 137
WEAK 315
weave down the road 375
WEDDING 423
Wednesday 322, 329
WEEK 326
weekly 326
WEIGH 215
WEIGHT 215
WEIRD 5
west 161
wet 405
What's happening? 493
WHAT? 183
WHEN? 180
WHERE? 183
WHICH 333
which one? 333
while 174
while ago 262
WHISKEY 321
WHITE 459
white faced 459
WHO? 183
WHO? 369
WHY? 8
WHY? 404
WIDE 473
wife 245, 248, 500
WILL 360
WIN 457
WINDOW 259
WINE 437
WINTER 272
WISE 21
WISH 165
WITH 476
without 476
wolf 483
woman 500
WONDERFUL 140
won't 58
WOOD 141
WORD 252
WORK 86
work 122
worker 86
WORLD 499
WORRY 357
WORTH 343
worthless 306
WOW! 81
wreck 325
WRITE 359
WRONG 243
wrong 302

X

xerox 47

Y

YEAR 349
yearly 497

yellow 353
YES 76
yesterday 104

yet 278
YOU 403
YOUR 469

yours 469
yourself 87
yourselves 87

Sign Language Flash Cards

by

Harry W. Hoemann,
&
Shirley A. Hoemann

1

AIRPLANE

The dominant hand, palm down, with the thumb, index finger, and little finger extended, is moved briefly forward twice in neutral space. This tense, reduplicated movement is used for the noun. A single, smooth movement in neutral space is the verb, FLY. FLY may be executed as a directional verb, with its origin and destination governed by the spatial organization of locations in context. Since the handshape for AIRPLANE can serve as a classifier, it can represent a number of verbs of motion: TAKE-OFF, LAND, CRASH, BANK, CLIMB, DO-STUNTS. TAKE-OFF, LAND, and CRASH may use the non-dominant palm as a base, or they may be executed in neutral space.

2

NOW, PRESENT

The two hands, palms up, are brought downward to a full stop as BENT B hands in neutral space. **Y** hands may be used. This sign is the temporal adverb used to mark the present tense. It is also used in several compounds: NOW + DAY = TODAY, NOW + NIGHT = TONIGHT, NOW + MORNING = THIS MORNING, NOW + WEEK = THIS WEEK, NOW + MONTH = THIS MONTH, NOW + YEAR = THIS YEAR.

3

DIRTY

The dominant hand is held with the back of the hand in contact with the underside of the chin, and the fingers of the hand, palm down, are wiggled briefly. If the **B** hand is placed similarly under the chin and the fingers make a small, circular, rooting movement, the sign is PIG.

4

KING

The right **K** hand touches the left shoulder and the right hip. If signed left-handed, the right shoulder and left hip are touched. The sign is believed to be motivated by a sash worn across the body by ancient nobility. The same sign is initialized with other handshapes for other royal dignitaries: **Q** for QUEEN, **P** for PRINCE, **L** for LORD, and **C** for CHRIST. PRINCESS may require the female gender marker (the thumb stroked on the jaw) along with the initialized PRINCE, although at least in Ohio the orientation of the P hand on the shoulder marks the differences in gender: the flat P hand against the shoulder for PRINCE, and the fingertips of the P hand touched to the shoulder for PRINCESS.

5

ODD, PECULIAR, STRANGE, WEIRD

The right C hand is held to the right side of the face, palm facing left, and it is moved across the face toward the left. As it crosses the face, the wrist is bent sharply so that the palm is turned downward. If the sign is executed left-handed, the orientations and movement are opposite.

6

KIND, KINDNESS

The BENT B hands, palms down, are rolled over one another in an alternating movement as they are brought down from the face forward from the body in neutral space. This sign does not translate *kind* in the sense of *sort*

7

WASTE

The back of dominant **BABY O** hand is placed into the non-dominant palm, fingers pointing forward, as in MONEY. The dominant hand is moved forward in a swift action as it opens into a **5** hand, as if scattering money in all directions. Other signs related to MONEY in addition to WASTE are BUY (the **BABY O** hand is placed in the nondominant palm and then moved forward from the body), SHOP (a reduplicated BUY with the hands moving laterally in space), EXPENSIVE (the dominant **5** hand moving laterally in space), EXPENSIVE (the dominant **5** hand is followed by WOW: the dominant **5** hand is shaken at the side of the body near the waist), and RICH (MONEY followed by a vertical execution of MUCH: the cupped hands drawn apart from each other, palms facing).

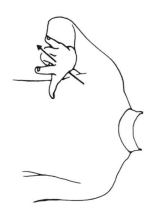

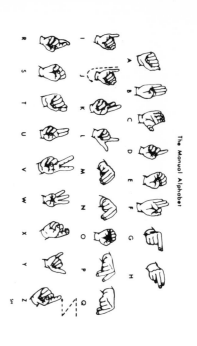

The Manual Alphabet

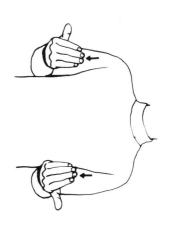

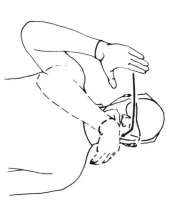

8 — WHY?

The **B** hand is held near the forehead with the palm facing the forehead. As the hand is moved forward, the handshape changes to a **Y** hand with the palm still facing the head. An alternative execution holds the **Y** hand some distance from the head, palm facing the head, and the middle three fingers are wiggled repeatedly. The sign WHY? is often used as a rhetorical question, substituting for a causal clause: HE STAY HOME; WHY? SICK. *He stayed home because he was sick.*

9 — RAIN

The **CLAW** hands or **5** hands, palms down, are stroked downward two or more times in neutral space, represents streams of raindrops. The sign is usually a compound, WATER (the hand is brought near the lips, but without detailing the **W** handshape) + RAIN. The sign may be modified to represent DRIVING RAIN or a LIGHT SPRINKLE. If the dominant hand references the chest, for WHITE, and then both hands flutter downward, the sign is SNOW.

10 — LAST-WEEK

The nondominant hand is held palm up in neutral space, and the dominant hand, index finger extended, is stroked outward across the other palm and, then, thrown back over the shoulder. The sign may be executed with the back of the dominant hand, index finger extended, stroked across the other palm and, then, moved back over the shoulder. If the dominant hand presents the numerals **2**, **3**, or **4** the meaning is changed to TWO-WEEKS-AGO, THREE-WEEKS-AGO, or FOUR-WEEKS-AGO. If, instead of throwing the hand back over the shoulder, the movement is forward in neutral space, the sign is NEXT-WEEK, TWO-WEEKS-FROM-NOW, THREE-WEEKS-FROM-NOW, or FOUR-WEEKS-FROM-NOW.

11 — MEDICINE

The middle fingertip of the dominant hand makes small circles in the center of the other palm. In some contexts the sign is POISON.

12 — HOPE, EXPECT

The dominant hand is brought toward the forehead, referencing THINK (but without detailing the handshape of the execution); then both hands are held off to the side, palms facing, as the fingers are bent towards each other one or more times. An alternative execution wiggles the fingers of both hands as the second syllable of the sign. HOPE is also executed as a natural gesture of crossing the fingers of both hands and agitating them with an appropriate facial expression.

13 — PATIENT

The thumb nail of the **A** hand, thumb up, is pressed to the chin as the head is bowed slightly. An alternative version rubs the thumb nail downward two or more times on the chin. This sign does not translate *patient* in the sense of a patient or client of a doctor or hospital. If the right hand is twisted at the wrist or rocked back and forth as the thumb presses against the chin with a pained facial expression, the sign is SUFFER, HURT.

14 — KNOW

The fingertips of the dominant hand are tapped on the forehead. The forehead is the locus of several signs involving mental activity, including THINK (the index finger tapped to the forehead), UNDERSTAND (the index finger flicked upward at the forehead), and FORGET (the dominant hand wipes the forehead with a lateral movement). If the fingertips of the dominant hand are touched to the forehead and then turned outward with a twist of the wrist, this is DON'T KNOW, an example of negative incorporation.

15 — ABOVE, OVER

The fingertips of the dominant hand are touched to the back of the nondominant hand or fist, and they are then raised upward in a spiral movement. An alternative execution circles the dominant hand in space above the other fist or above the back of the other hand. The nondominant hand provides a point of reference, and the meaning is conveyed by the relation of the dominant hand to the other hand. If the dominant hand is lowered beneath the other hand or circled under it, the sign is BELOW, UNDER.

16 — FROM

The nondominant index finger is raised upward in neutral space, and the curved index finger of the dominant hand is drawn away from the other index finger and toward the body. The nondominant hand provides a point of reference, and the meaning is conveyed by the action of the dominant hand in relation to the other hand.

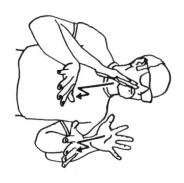

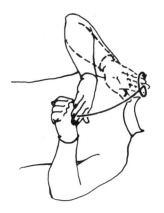

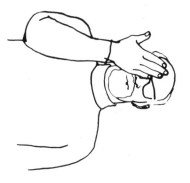

BROWN

The **B** hand, palm facing forward, is brushed downward along the cheek one or more times. This same execution may mean BEER in some regions of the country.

PERSON, AGENT

The two hands, palms facing or turned toward the body, are brought downward along the sides of the body near the waist. The sign may occur as a suffix with certain nouns or verbs: LAW + AGENT = LAWYER, TEACH + AGENT = TEACHER, JAIL + AGENT = PRISONER, LEARN + AGENT = STUDENT. The sign may be initialized with **P** hands for PERSON.

MAYBE, PERHAPS

Both hands are held palms up in neutral space. They are moved alternately up and down indecisively, usually with a dubious facial expression or with shrugged shoulders. Related signs are JUDGE, made with **F** hands, palms facing, and DOUBT, made with **S** hands, palms down.

SICK

The middle fingertip of the dominant hand is touched to the forehead, and the middle fingertip of the nondominant hand is touched to the stomach. The sign may be made with the dominant hand only. There is an idiomatic expression in ASL, SICK YOU, which is translated, *You make me sick.* This sign may be inflected with an elliptical orbit and reduplication for CHRONICALLY ILL, with fast reduplication for REPEATEDLY ILL, or with an intensive flourish for VERY ILL.

WISE

The curved index finger, tip pointing downward, is moved downward in front of the forehead two or more times. The sign may be motivated by the notion of plumbing the depths of an intelligent mind. Signed with the **P** hand, the sign is PHILOSOPHY.

LADY

The thumb of the **5** hand is brushed along the chin and touched to the chest. Contact with the chin references the female gender region, and the **5** hand touched to the chest may be motivated by a lacy blouse. A related sign, GENTLEMAN, is executed by referencing the forehead (the male gender region) and then touching the chest. These signs typically introduce a formal address, LADIES AND GENTLEMEN.

RUN

The nondominant hand is held, palm up, in neutral space, and the dominant hand, palm down, makes short, brushing movements as both hands move forward from the body. This sign is used with animate subjects, such as a person or animal. It is not used with inanimate subjects, like an engine or a computer program. It does not translate the English word, *run* in all of its possible contexts, such as a *run* in a stocking, a *run* on a bank, a *runny nose*, a home *run*, *etc.*

UNDERSTAND

The index finger is flicked upward from the fist as the hand is held near the forehead, palm toward the forehead. The flicking action may be reduplicated. A head nod may accompany the execution.

TRAIN, RAILROAD

The fingers of the dominant **H** hand, palm down, are rubbed back and forth on the back of the extended fingers of the nondominant **H** hand, palm down. The underlying metaphor is something moving on tracks.

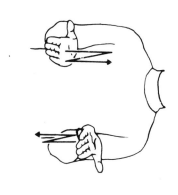 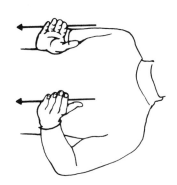 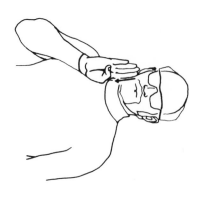

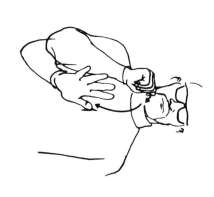 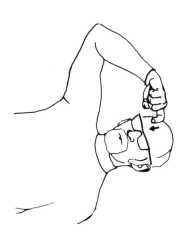 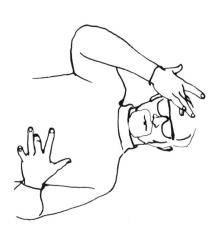

 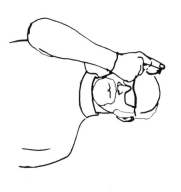 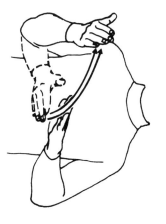

PLAY

The **Y** hands are held, palms toward the body, and the hands are moved up and down simultaneously in front of the body, bending at the wrists. The movement may be alternating instead of simultaneous. This sign does not translate *play, drama*. A related sign, PARTY, swings the **Y** hands back and forth in neutral space, palms facing. **P** hands may be used.

SMELL

The fingertips of the dominant hand are brought toward the nose repeatedly in a natural gesture imitating the act of smelling something. This sign does not translate *smell, stink*, which is generally indicated by means of the universal gesture of holding the nose with the thumb and index finger.

BECOME

The dominant hand, palm up, is held under the nondominant hand, palm down, in neutral space. The hands are turned over as they exchange positions. In one version the hands are cupped and separated, in another they are flat and in slight contact.

CALL, SUMMON

The nondominant hand or fist is held palm down in neutral space. The fingers of the dominant hand are slapped against the back of the nondominant hand, and the dominant hand is then brought back toward the shoulder in the **A** position. The sign is the first element of at least two compounds: WARN (SUMMON + a natural gesture of wagging the index finger) and INVITE (SUMMON followed by a movement of the palm up dominant hand toward the midsection of the speaker's body). The sign does not translate *call, shout* or *call, telephone*.

BEFORE, PREVIOUSLY

The nondominant palm is turned out, away from the body, and the dominant hand, palm toward the body, is drawn from an initial position in contact with the back of the nondominant hand toward the speaker's body. A related sign, AFTERWARD, places the nondominant hand in neutral space with the palm toward the speaker's body, and the dominant hand moves forward in neutral space after touching the back of the nondominant hand. Ordinarily these signs refer to time, but they may also mean ON THIS SIDE or ON THAT SIDE. The nondominant hand can provide a frame of reference for a number of variations with the same motivation: ON THE LEFT SIDE, ON THE RIGHT SIDE, ON EITHER SIDE, IN FRONT OF, and IN BACK OF.

CHEMISTRY, SCIENCE

The **A** hands, thumbs extended downward, are alternately moved downward in small circles in neutral space. The sign is used for SCIENCE in general or, specifically, for CHEMISTRY. Followed by the AGENT suffix, the sign is SCIENTIST or CHEMIST.

SLEEP

The **5** hand is drawn downward across the face as the eyes close, ending in the **O** position. Its antonym, AWAKEN, is signed with the thumb and index fingers of both hands at the sides of the closed eyes. The fingers spread apart slowly as the eyes are opened. An alternative sign SLEEP uses the palm of the hand to represent a pillow, and the head is tilted so as to rest against the palm with the eyes closed.

JOIN

The open **F** hands are linked together in neutral space as the thumbs and index fingers close. The sign may be executed directionally, linking the speaker with an object. If the linked **F** hands are circled counterclockwise, horizontally in neutral space, the sign is COOPERATE. If the **F** hands are linked together repeatedly in alternating positions as the hands move vertically or horizontally through neutral space, the sign is CHAIN. The sign, JOIN, may be executed in reverse to imply the opposite, SEPARATE.

MANY

The two **A** hands, palms up or facing the speaker, are thrown upward so as to end as two **5** hands, palms toward the speaker. The execution is often reduplicated. If the final position is held with a questioning facial expression, the sign is HOW MANY? or, in some contexts, HOW MUCH DOES IT COST? The interrogative is usually executed with only one hand.

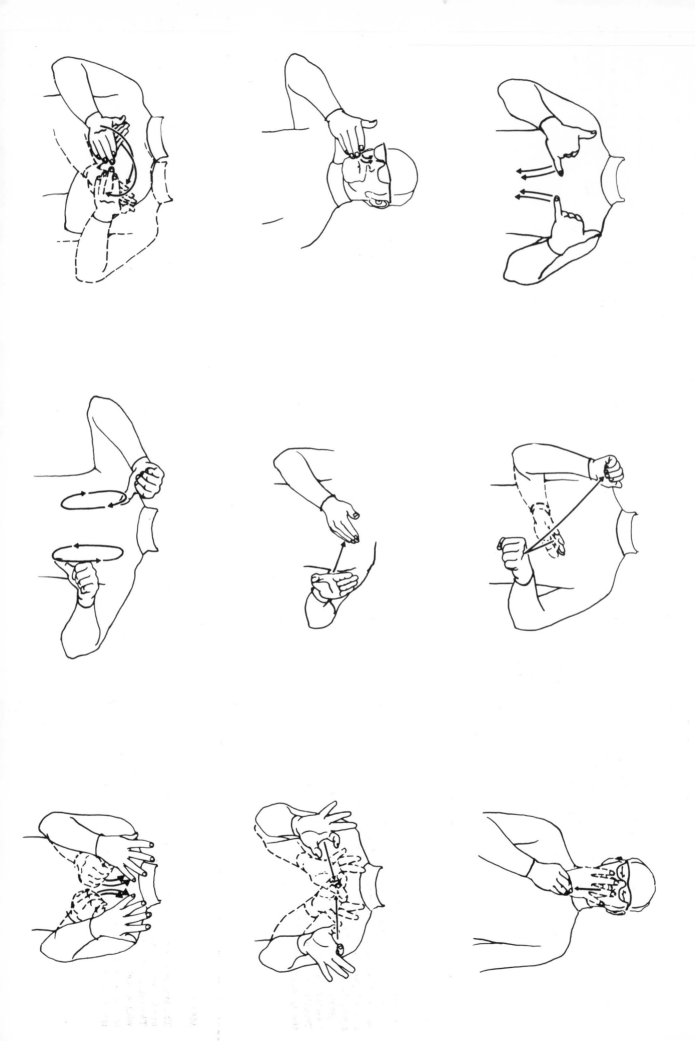

SEARCH, SEEK, LOOK FOR   35

The C hand is held near the eyes, and small circles are traced in neutral space in a vertical plane. The sign may be accompanied by eye and head movements associated with looking for something or searching for something. This may be an initialized sign from the French, *cherchez*.

PRINCIPAL

The **P** hand is circled in a horizontal plane in neutral space and then brought down so that the tip of the middle finger of the **P** hand touches the back of the nondominant fist. This sign refers to the *principal* of a school. It does not translate the adjective, *principal, chief, main*.

MORE   38

The clustered fingertips of both **BABY O** hands are touched together one or more times in neutral space. To imply adding **MORE** on top of what is already there, the dominant **BABY O** hand may make an arc and then come into contact with the clustered fingertips of the other hand. A related sign, ADD, brings the dominant **5** hand up and under the nondominant **5** hand, and both hands' fingertips are clustered together as they come into contact in neutral space, the dominant hand under the nondominant hand. And alternative sign for ADD holds the nondominant **H** hand, palm down, in neutral space, and the extended fingers of the dominant **H** hand are brought up and over with a twist of the wrist so as to come to rest on the extended fingers of the nondominant hand.

TAX, CHARGE, FINE, PRICE, COST   36

The nondominant hand is held in a horizontal plane in neutral space, palm toward the body. The dominant **X** hand, palm to the side, is swung down so that the curled index finger strikes the inside of the other palm as it passes.

ABOUT   39

The nondominant **BABY O** hand is held in neutral space with the clustered fingers pointing toward the dominant hand, and the index finger of the dominant hand makes a circle around the clustered fingertips of the nondominant hand, coming to rest on top of them. AROUND is executed similarly, except the clustered fingertips of the nondominant hand point upward, and a clockwise circle is made around them in a horizontal plane.

CURIOUS, CURIOSITY   37

The thumb and index finger of the **F** hand pinch the skin of the throat near the Adam's apple as the hand is agitated slightly. In Northwest Ohio this is the sign FROG.

PLEASE, LIKE   42

The hand is rubbed in a circular movement over the heart. The sign may be used as a verb, LIKE, and the verb, PLEASE. It also occurs as an imperative, PLEASE. If both hands are rubbed over the chest and stomach, the sign is ENJOY, PLEASURE. An alternative sign, LIKE, draws the open **F** hand forward from the chest, closing the thumb and index finger as the hand moves forward from the body.

SHORT   40

The dominant hand, palm down, is brought down to a full stop at about waist level. Combined with a gender marker, the sign may mean BOY or GIRL. This sign is the opposite of TALL, which is executed similarly but at head height These signs, SHORT and TALL, refer only to stature. They do not translate *short* in the sense of *a short time* or *a short story*, or *tall* in the sense of *a tall tale*.

COOKIE   43

The fingertips of the **CLAW** hand are touched lightly on the nondominant palm twice as the hand is twisted at the wrist. The sign imitates the use of a cookie cutter to cut cookies from a sheet of pastry.

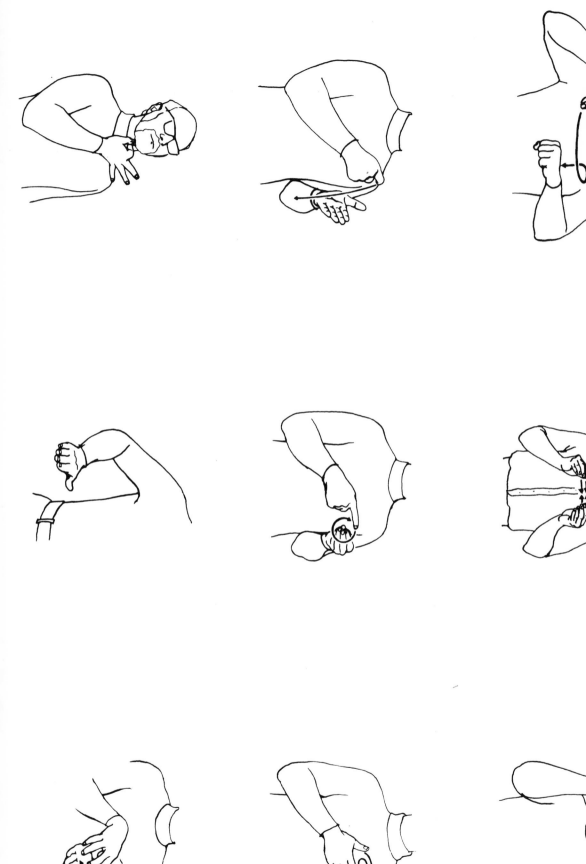
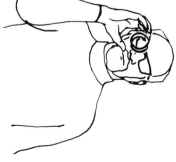

44 PLACE

The **P** hands trace a circle or rectangle in a horizontal plane in neutral space, beginning at the midline some distance from the body and moving apart, then toward the body, and then toward the midline. The sign may be executed with index fingers. An alternative sign AREA, PLACE circles the dominant **A** hand above the nondominant **A** hand, ending with the thumb landing on the thumb nail of the nondominant hand.

45 OPPOSITE, OPPOSED

The index fingers of both hands are pointed toward each other in neutral space, and they are jerked apart with a slight twist of both wrists. Followed by AGENT sign, it is ENEMY. Preceded by THINK, the sign is DISAGREE. If the hands are moved back and forth with tensed muscles as the index fingers point toward each other, this is the verb, STRUGGLE.

46 AND

The right **5** hand is held in neutral space with the palm facing left. The hand is moved toward the right as the fingertips are clustered together. The sign represents taking something from the left and bringing it to the right so as to connect it up. If the sign is executed with the left hand, the orientation and movement are reversed.

47 COPY ME, IMITATE MY SIGNS

The nondominant hand is held with the palm toward the body, and the fingertips of the dominant **5** hand are brushed lightly against the back of the nondominant hand as they move forward from the body and close into the **BABY O** handshape. This instruction precedes group signing as in the *Pledge of Allegiance* or a religious hymn or prayer. For the related sign, COPY, MAKE A COPY, the dominant hand begins away from the body, closing from the **5** to the **BABY O** handshape as it makes contact with the nondominant palm in neutral space. PHOTOCOPY, XEROX holds the nondominant hand palm down, and the movement of the dominant hand is downward in space.

48 FEAR, AFRAID

The **A** hands are held in neutral space some distance apart with the thumbs up. They are brought forcefully together at the midline opening into **5** hands and crossing at the wrists as they do so, ending with the palms of the **5** hands shielding the body from harm. An alternative execution quivers the overlapping **5** hands in neutral space, palms toward the body.

49 COMFORT, COMFORTABLE

The palms of each hand are rubbed over the back of the other hand, alternately. The action imitates warming one's hands at a fire.

50 DON'T, NO

The wrists are crossed in front of the face with the palms facing outward. The hands are drawn apart forcefully. This is a strong negation, suggesting prohibition, refusal, or denial. It is often an imperative. The sign may be executed with the palms down in neutral space.

51 SON

The dominant hand begins near the forehead, referencing the male gender region, and then drops, palm up, into the palm of the nondominant hand. The sign is a compound derived from MALE + BABY. DAUGHTER begins near the chin and then drops, palm up, into the palm of the nondominant hand. It is a compound derived from FEMALE + BABY.

52 OPEN

The **B** hands, index fingers touching and pointing upward or forward, are turned with a twist of the wrist so that the palms of both hands face each other. The opposite action is CLOSE, SHUT. There is an idiom in ASL, SLEEP CLOSE, which is translated *Sleep tight*. Either sign, OPEN or CLOSE, may be executed in a vertical or horizontal orientation; the choice sometimes depends on what it is that is being opened or closed.

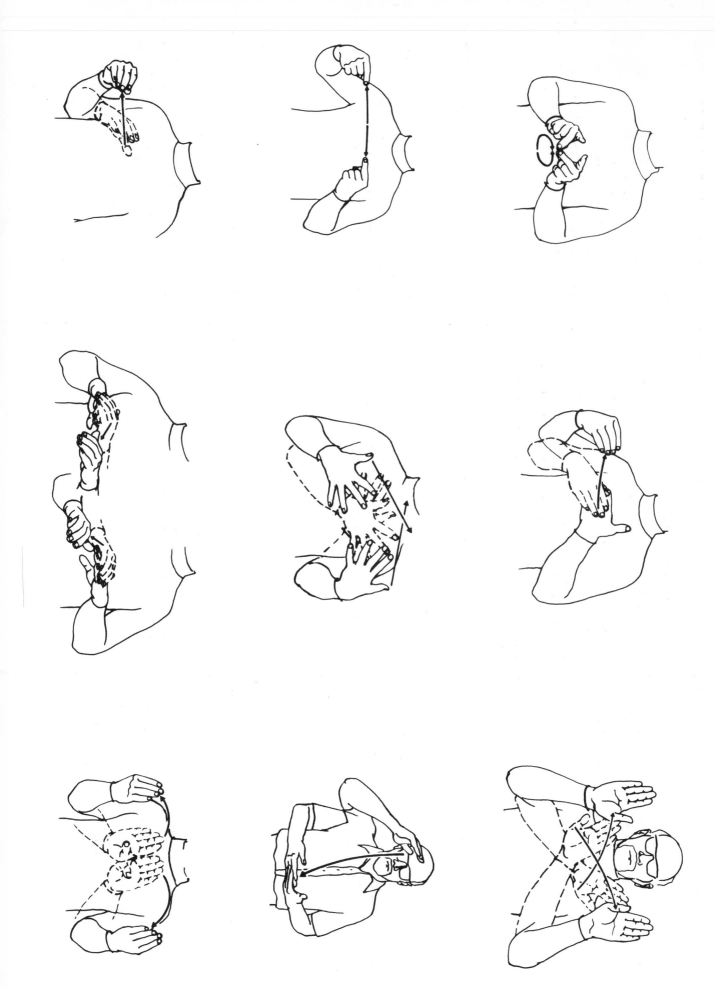

53 VOTE, ELECT

The nondominant O hand is held in neutral space with the opening facing up, representing the opening of a ballot box, and the thumb and index finger of the dominant F hand are thrust into the opening as if dropping in a ballot.

54 ADVISE, COUNSEL

The nondominant fist is held, palm down, in a neutral position. The fingertips of the dominant 5 hand are brushed over the top of the fist, as if taking information from it, and, then, thrown forward from the body, as if giving the information to someone. Followed by the AGENT sign, the execution is COUNSELOR, ADVISOR.

55 CUP

The nondominant hand is held, palm up, in neutral space, and the dominant C hand, representing a cylindrical object, is placed on the palm. The sign is an example of a *Classifier* that has become a conventional sign. Since it can be executed as a classifier, it can indicate the number or relative position of cups. If the nondominant C hand serves as a reference, the dominant C hand can move laterally to indicate a row of cups or even several rows of cups. A related sign, GLASS, is distinguished from CUP by moving the C hand upward from the nondominant palm, suggesting a taller container.

56 BREAD

The outside edge of the BENT B hand or the fingertips of the BENT B hand make slicing motions on the back of the fingers of the nondominant BENT B hand, palm toward the body. The sign is said to be motivated by the European method of cradling a loaf of bread in the left arm while slicing it with a knife.

57 PRAISE

The fingertips of the hand are brought near the lips and then the hands are clapped together in a natural gesture of applause. In casual usage, the hand clapping may occur without the reference to the lips.

58 MONKEY

The fingertips of the C or CLAW hands scratch the sides as they are brushed upward several times. The sign imitates the posture and scratching commonly seen in chimpanzees.

59 REBEL, DISOBEY

The S hand, fingers toward the face, is jerked off to the side with a twist of the elbow and wrist, ending with the fingers facing outward. The head is often turned away from the S hand as the sign is executed. A related sign, REFUSE, WON'T, jerks the thumb up A hand back over the shoulder with a similar turning of the head.

60 SOME

The nondominant hand is held, palm up, in neutral space, and the little finger edge of the dominant B hand cuts a curved portion off the fingertips of the other hand. This sign may be combined with the numeral ONE in the compound SOMEONE or with THING in SOMETHING.

61 MOVIE, MOTION PICTURE

The dominant 5 hand is rubbed back and forth horizontally against the palm of the nondominant 5 hand. The sign is motivated by the flickering light once associated with movies. An alternative sign rests the heel of the dominant 5 hand, palm facing outward, on the back of the nondominant hand or fist, and the dominant hand is wagged back and forth gently. Still another sign, motivated by hand-operated cameras, holds the left palm in neutral space, fingers up and palm to the right, and the right fist makes a circular movement on the palm, imitating the motion of the crank.

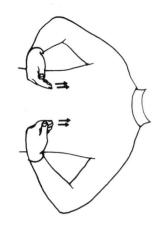 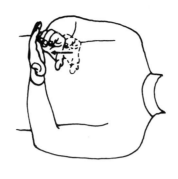 

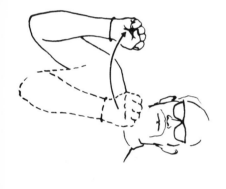 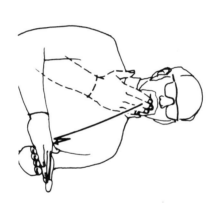 

 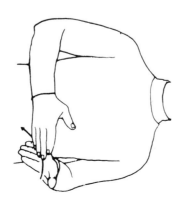 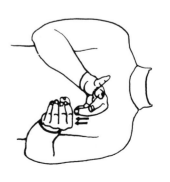

62 NEED, SHOULD, MUST, OUGHT

The **X** hand, palm down, is moved sharply downward in neutral space. The sign may be reduplicated. The sign implies any kind of necessity or obligation, with the degree indicated by the relative forcefulness of the execution and by the accompanying nonmanual features, especially facial expression.

63 TIRED

The fingertips of the **BENT B** hands are touched to the body just above the waist, and the hands are collapsed and rolled forward so that the backs of the fingers are in contact with the body. The body may slump as the sign is executed.

64 MEAT

The nondominant hand is held in neutral space with the palm toward the body. The dominant **F** hand pinches the fleshy part of the nondominant hand between the thumb and index finger. The hands may be agitated in neutral space briefly. A related sign, GRAVY, is executed below the nondominant hand, as the thumb and index finger of the dominant **F** hand slide off the edge of the nondominant hand.

65 DIRT, GROUND, SOIL

The fingertips of both hands are rubbed against the thumbs in neutral space as if rubbing dirt between them. The sign may be executed with one hand. This sign is not used for the adjective, DIRTY.

66 THIRSTY

The fingertip of the dominant hand is stroked downward on the throat one or more times. A related sign, SWALLOW, draws the raised, dominant index finger down the throat, beginning at the chin.

67 DRY

The dominant **X** hand, palm down, is drawn across the chin. The sign may begin with the index finger extended, changing to the **X** handshape as the sign is executed. An alternative execution for DRY, BORING, draws the dominant **B** hand, palm down, across the chin, ending in the **S** handshape. A very slow, deliberate execution is VERY DRY.

68 RIGHT, CORRECT, EXACT

Both hands are held in neutral space, index fingers extended, and the dominant hand is brought down forcefully so that the fist strikes the other and glances back. A reduplicated execution with the dominant hand making repeated contact with the top of the other fist is REGULARLY. Both hands may move forward in space as the dominant hand is REGULARLY is executed, or the dominant hand may make small circles above the other hand as the reduplicated executions occur. Executed with **P** or **F** hands, the sign is PERFECT, EXACT. The closed fingertips of the **P** or **F** hand make contact as the sign is executed.

69 SKILLED, EXPERT

The right hand grasps the outer edge of the left hand, palm facing right and fingers are pointing upward, and the right hand slides off the left hand and closes as it is pulled forward in neutral space. If the sign is executed left handed, the right hand serves as the nondominant hand, and the palm faces left. The sign is considered to be highly complimentary. It may be executed forcefully with an intense facial expression (pinched lips squinted eyes, and cocked head). An alternative sign with a similar field of meaning brings the closed fingers of the dominant **F** hand into contact with the right chin with a decisive movement.

70 IGNORE

The dominant **4** hand is brought near the nose and then moved forward from the face into neutral space. An alternative execution moves the **4** hand to the side and downward in neutral space with a forceful gesture. This second execution is similar to the sign LOUSY, which requires the **3** hand. The execution of IGNORE may be directed toward a locus associated with its object.

 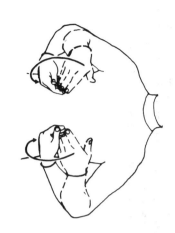 

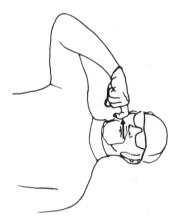  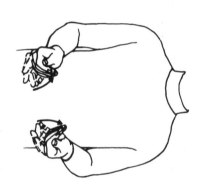

STUBBORN, MULISH 71

The thumb of the dominant hand is touched to the side of the forehead, and the fingers are bent forcefully forward in one quick movement. The sign may be derived from the sign MULE, which places the B hand against the side of the forehead and bends it forward several times, imitating the movement of a mule's ears. MULE may be executed with both hands.

EGG 72

The H hands are held with the palms toward the body, and the extended fingers are brought downward in arcs with twists of the wrists as if breaking an egg. An alternate sign holds an imaginary egg in the dominant hand, breaks it against an imaginary surface, and then opens it in neutral space.

PUNISH, PUNISHMENT 74

The nondominant forearm is held in neutral space, palm down, at about a 60 degree angle, and the right index finger of the dominant hand is swung downward so as to strike the outside of the other forearm near the elbow. The lips are often pinched as the sign is executed.

CAN, BE ABLE, ABILITY 75

The A hands or S hands, palms facing downward, are brought downward to a full stop with a forceful gesture in neutral space. An alternate sign holds the S hands, palms facing, in neutral space and moves them up and down with a slight lateral movement, ending with an abrupt stop, muscles tensed. The sign is related to the adjective, STRONG, which clenches the fists, tenses the muscles, and jerks the fists slightly downward to a full stop.

STORE 77

The BABY O hands are held with the clustered fingers pointing downward, and the fingers are moved slightly forward and backward by bending at the wrists. The sign may be motivated by the action of a sales person holding up a garment and shaking it out for a buyer's inspection. The verb, SELL, is executed as a single, smooth movement. The noun, STORE, is reduplicated and tensed. The noun may refer to a PEDDLER, that is, a deaf person or impersonator who sells pencils or alphabet cards in shopping centers or from door to door. The deaf community generally disapproves of peddling.

ANY 78

The A hand, thumb up, is drawn downward and off to the side with the thumb trailing. The sign must be distinguished from OTHER, which moves the thumb-up A hand off to the side in an arc, with the thumb in an upright position at all times. The sign ANY is the first element of the compounds, ANY + ONE and ANY + THING.

PREPARE, ARRANGE, PLAN 79

The two hands, palms facing, are held off to the left in neutral space, fingers pointing forward. They are moved to the right in a series of short steps as if arranging something in order on a table. An alternate execution sweeps the hand smoothly from left to right in neutral space. The sign may be initialized with P hands to represent the English word, *prepare* or with R hands to represent *ready*.

YES 76

The A or Y hand is moved in a nodding motion in neutral space. Various shades of meaning associated with an affirmation or assent may be indicated by the accompanying facial expression or body language. A nod of the head may signal agreement or assent without any accompanying sign.

LEVEL, EVEN, EQUAL, FAIR 73

The BENT B hands are held in front of the body, palms down, and the fingertips are touched together one or more times so as to form a flat surface out of the backs of the fingers of both hands. The sign represents a LEVEL or EVEN surface, but it can also be EVEN in the sense of an EQUAL amount and, therefore, FAIR. A directional execution with a hostile facial expression is GET EVEN.

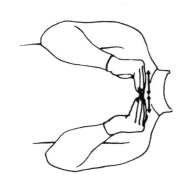

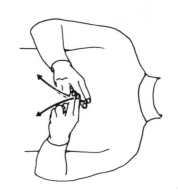

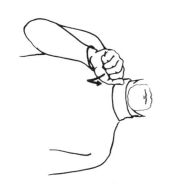

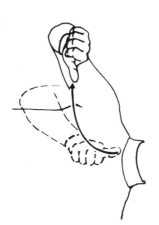

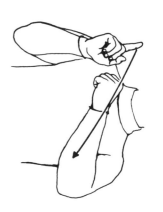

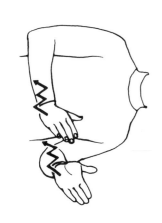

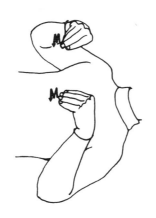

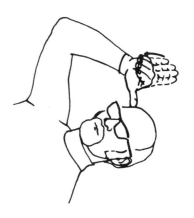

80 LIKE, BE ATTRACTED TO

The **5** hand is touched against the chest, and the hand is brought forward from the body as the fingers close into the closed **F** position, palm toward the body. A two-handed execution of the sign is INTERESTED. The sign does not translate *like* in the sense of *same, similar*. An alternate sign LIKE rubs the palm in a small circle on the chest or over the heart.

81 WOW! PHEW!

The **5** hand is shaken vigorously at the side of the body. This sign occurs as the second element in several compounds: MONEY + WOW = EXPENSIVE, TOUCH + WOW = HOT TO THE TOUCH, CLEVER + WOW = VERY INTELLI-GENT. The sign may also be used alone as a sympathetic response to bad or good news.

82 STUDY

The nondominant hand is held, palm up, in neutral space. The fingers of the dominant **5** hand are directed toward the other palm and wiggled. An alternative execution flicks the fingers of the **BABY O** hand toward the other palm several times, open-ing them into a **5** hand with each movement. Related signs include NOTICE (touching the tip of the index finger into the nondominant palm), INVESTIGATE (moving the tip of the index finger forward two or more times in the nondominant palm), RESEARCH (an initialized version of INVESTIGATE), and EMPHASIZE (pressing the ball of the thumb in the palm of the nondominant hand).

83 FAT

The **C** hands, palms facing the cheeks, are drawn outward from the cheeks. The cheeks may be puffed out as the sign is executed. An alternative sign holds the curved **5** hands at the sides of the body and moves them outward. In this case, too, the cheeks may be puffed out as the sign is executed. The antonyms, THIN, are signed by drawing the thumb and index finger narrowly down the cheeks at the sides of the mouth, indicating a thin face, or by drawing the palms of both hands narrowly down the sides of the body, indicating a thin body.

84 SWEETHEART

The **A** hands, thumbs up, are placed together with the backs of the fingers touching, and the thumbs are wiggled toward each other in a parallel motion.

85 LIST

The nondominant palm is held in neutral space with the fingers upright, and the **BENT B** on the dominant hand makes small steps down the left palm, either with the fingertips or with the little finger edge. The verb, MAKE A LIST, is executed simi-larly, but the fingertips of the dominant **BABY O** hand place items on the other palm in small steps moving downward on the palm. The sign is related to CHAPTER, in which the edge of the **BENT B** hand marks off the top and bottom of CHAPTER on the nondominant palm, and PARAGRAPH, in which a span is marked off on the nondominant palm with the thumb and fingertips of the **C** hand.

86 WORK

Both hands form fists, and the wrist of the dominant hand is struck repeatedly against the back of the other fist. The dom-inant hand may be swung back and forth in an arc between contacts. The latter execution with **B** hands is BUSINESS. The **D** hand tapped against the back of the nondominant fist is DUTY. WORK + AGENT is WORKER. An alternative sign WORK agitates the curved **5** hands, palms down, in neutral space.

87 MYSELF

The **A** hand, thumb up, is touched against the chest one or more times. This handshape is characteristic of all the reflexive pronouns. They are executed directionally: YOURSELF toward the listener, HIMSELF, HERSELF, and ITSELF toward the referent, OURSELVES on the right and left shoulder, YOURSELVES (plural) in a sweeping movement or in a series of discrete movements that include the listeners, and THEM-SELVES in a sweeping movement or a series of discrete move-ments directed toward the referents.

88 HURRY

The **H** hands, palms facing and fingers pointing forward, are moved forward from the body in parallel movements consisting of short hops.

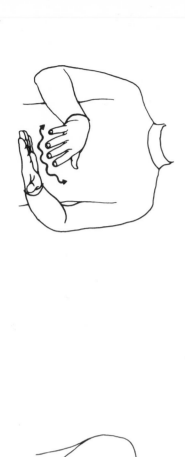

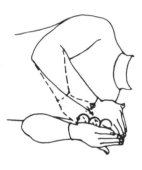
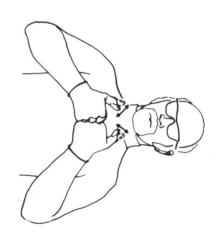

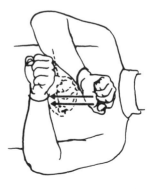

89

ELECTRIC, ELECTRICITY

The two **X** hands are touched together two or more times at the second joint as the hands are held in a horizontal plane in neutral space. A related sign executed with **BENT V hands** and a slight twist of the wrist between contacts is PHYSICS.

90

INTERPRET

The **F** hands are placed in opposing positions in neutral space, one hand above the other, palms facing. The are rocked alternately back and forth with twists of the wrists. The sign is commonly used for the role of interpreting from English to Sign or Sign to English. Executed with the AGENT sign, it is INTERPRETER.

91

BRING, CARRY

The hands are held, palms up, in neutral space, slightly off to the side. They are brought to the front of the body in a gesture that implies carrying a tray. Followed by the AGENT sign, it is WAITER, WAITRESS, or SERVANT.

92

SWEET, SUGAR, CANDY, CUTE

The fingertips of the dominant hand are touched to the chin and stroked downward. The execution may be reduplicated. The sign refers to sweet food, but it may also be used metaphorically for a sweet disposition, and it sometimes is CUTE. It may be executed with the extended index and middle fingers.

93

DOCTOR, PHYSICIAN

The fingertips of the **M** or **D** hand are touched to the wrist at the place where the pulse is taken. Signed with the **N** hand, the sign is NURSE.

94

THAN

The nondominant **BENT B** hand is held in neutral space so that the fingers form a flat surface. The dominant hand, palm down, is brought downward in neutral space so that it strikes the tips of fingers of the other hand as it continues its downward course.

95

KEY, LOCK

The dominant **X** hand is twisted against the nondominant palm as if a KEY were turning in a LOCK. An alternative sign holds an imaginary key in the dominant hand and twists it either at the nondominant palm or in neutral space. This latter execution is the sign of choice for representing the action of START A CAR, that is, turn on the ignition.

96

VARIOUS, VARIETY

The index fingers of both hands are pointed forward, palms down, and they are wiggled up and down rapidly as the hands are brought out to the sides of the body. If the hands make larger up and down alternating movements as they are brought to the sides of the body, the sign is the verb, VARY.

97

DISCUSS, ARGUE

The index finger of the dominant hand is struck repeatedly into the palm of the nondominant hand. Executed with vigor, the sign can mean ARGUE, FIGHT. A discussion between two people can be represented by alternating the execution, first striking the left palm with the right index finger and, then, striking the right palm with the left index finger, repeating the action several times.

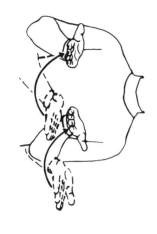  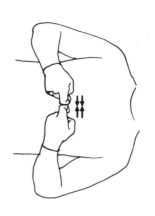

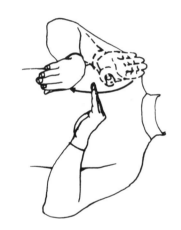 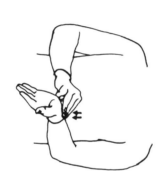 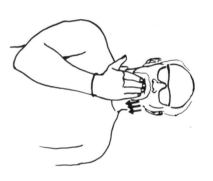

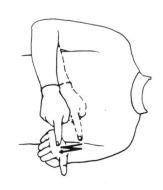 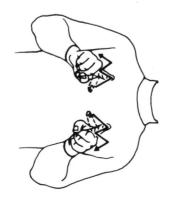 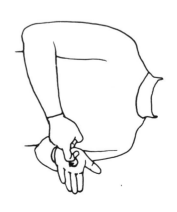

LEAVE, DEPART 98

The open hands, palms down, are moved to the side across the body, ending with closed hands off to the side of the body. An alternative sign holds the **5** hand, palm toward the face, in neutral space, and draws it forward from the face as the fingers close into the **BABY O** position. This latter sign may be executed directionally, moving toward the exit determined by the spatial organization of the discourse.

WASH CLOTHES 99

The fingers of the **A** hands are rubbed together in neutral space in a natural gesture associated with scrubbing. To represent a WASHING MACHINE, the curved **5** hands are placed, one on top of the other, palms facing, and they are twisted in opposite directions with twists of the wrists, representing the agitator in a washing machine.

HIDE, CONCEAL 100

The nondominant hand, palm down, provides a frame of reference. The thumbnail of the dominant **A** hand is pressed against the lips or chin, and the **A** hand is, then, moved downward and under the other palm. The nondominant palm may close over the **A** hand as it is moved under it. The first element of this sign, pressing the **A** hand against the lips, may be deleted.

EXCEED, TOO MUCH, EXCESS 101

The **BENT B** hands are held in neutral space, palms down, with the dominant hand above the nondominant hand. The dominant hand is then raised a considerable distance above the other hand and brought to a full stop. An exaggerated execution would be WAY TOO MUCH. An appropriate facial expression is likely to accompany the sign. Without the full stop the sign is EXCEEDING, IN EXCESS OF, OVER. If the hands in the initial position are brought forward to a full stop, or if the dominant hand slices forward over the other hand with a twist of its wrist to a full stop, the sign is LIMIT, LIMITED. By controlling the amount of space between the hands, one can vary the meaning from A SMALL AMOUNT to A GENEROUS AMOUNT.

DON'T CARE 102

The tip of the index finger is touched to the nose and then turned out and away from the face. It is related to the sign, IGNORE, executed with the **4** hand, and LOUSY, executed with the **3** hand.

CATHOLIC 103

The fingertips of the **H** hand trace a cross on the forehead or over the upper portion of the face. A similar execution with the **I** hand is ITALY.

TOMORROW 104

The **A** hand, thumb up, is moved forward in an arc along the cheek with a twist of the wrist. A reduplicated execution is DAILY, EVERY DAY. If the direction of movement is reversed, going back along the cheek, the sign is YESTERDAY, although another execution touches the thumb of the **A** or **Y** hand to the jaw and shoulder for YESTERDAY.

MACHINE, FACTORY 105

The **CLAW** hands are held in neutral space, palms toward the body, and they are brought downward two or more times so that their fingers intermesh like cog wheels. If a specific machine, such as a DRILL PRESS or TABLE SAW, needs to be referenced, sign mime and graphic depiction are likely to be added as a paraphrase.

SAD 106

The **5** hands are held with the palms toward the face, and they are brought downward gently as the head and shoulders are bowed slightly. The sign may be executed with one hand.

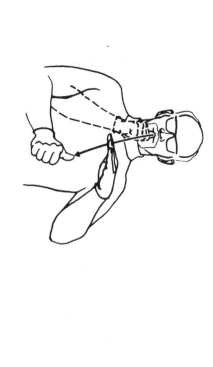

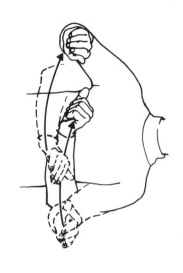

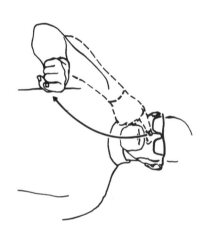

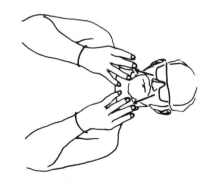
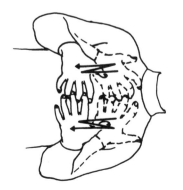

CONGRESS

The right C hand is touched to the right shoulder. The same sign with the L hand is LEGISLATURE. Executed with a B on the right shoulder and D on the left, the sign is BOARD. If these signs are executed left-handed, the positions are reversed.

STAR

The index finger of both hands is pointed upward, palms facing out, and the edges of the index fingers are brushed against each other as they pass alternately up and down in front of the body.

ICE CREAM, SOUP

The H hand, palm up, is dipped down into the nondominant hand, palm up, and raised to the mouth. The signs ICE CREAM and SOUP are signed similarly, although for SOUP the nondominant hand may be cupped so as to represent a bowl. The context will generally make clear which is meant. ICE CREAM may also be signed by licking an imaginary cone.

OLD

The C hand is closed into a fist as it is brought downward from the chin in a waving motion as if tugging or stroking a beard. In Northwest Ohio the sign is executed downward from the nose in front of the face. In Pennsylvania the open hand, palm down, is touched to the chest several times as it proceeds up the chest for AGE IN YEARS. Executed with a questioning facial expression, the Pennsylvania sign is *How old are you?*

BIRD

The back of the hand is held near the chin, and the thumb and index finger are touched together repeatedly, representing the beak of a bird. CHICKEN is signed similarly, but is often executed as a compound, BEAK + PECK IN THE HAND. An alternative sign CHICKEN scratches in the nondominant hand with the fingertips of the V hand. DUCK is signed like BIRD, but with the index and middle fingers touched to the thumb, representing the broader beak of a duck. EAGLE hooks the curved index finger forward and downward from the nose.

CLEAN, NICE

The nondominant hand is held palm up in neutral space, and the dominant hand, palm down, scrapes across the other palm, moving out from the body. Reduplicated the sign is CLEAN HOUSE, CLEAN UP. Initialized with the P hand, the sign is PURE.

BUG, BUGGY

The thumb of the 3 hand is touched to the nose as the fingers are wiggled. Preceded by FEEL, the sign is ITCH, TICKLE. An alternative sign for BUG, INSECT, links the little fingers of the 5 hands, palms down and wrists crossed, as the two hands make a crawling motion forward from the body.

SLOW, SLOWLY

The nondominant hand is held, palm down, in neutral space, and the fingertips of the dominant hand are drawn slowly up the back of the other hand toward the forearm. If the sign is executed very slowly and deliberately, the sign is VERY SLOW or VERY SLOWLY.

PICTURE

The right C hand partly circles the right eye, and it is then brought down so as to be placed against the left palm, which faces outward in neutral space. The first element of the sign may be deleted. A left-handed execution reverses the hands. To represent TAKE A PICTURE with a camera, an imaginary camera is held in the hands as the shutter is pressed.

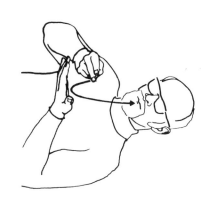 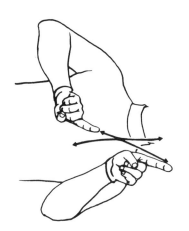 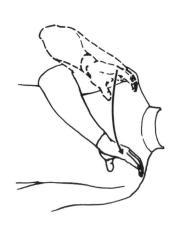

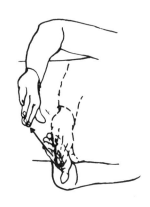  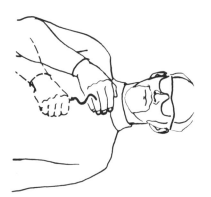

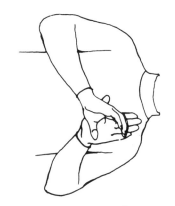 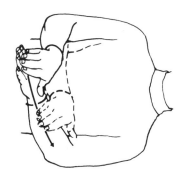 

FIRST, FIRST OF ALL

The left thumb is raised in neutral space, and the right index finger is struck against the ball of the thumb. If the right index finger strikes the index fingertip of the left L hand, the sign is SECOND or SECONDLY. If it strikes the tip of the middle finger of the left 3 hand, the sign is THIRD or THIRDLY. If it strikes the little fingertip of the left 4 hand, the sign is FOURTH or FOURTHLY. The hands are reversed for left-handed executions.

INSTEAD OF, EXCHANGE, TRADE

The F hands are held in a horizontal plane, fingers pointing forward, with one hand slightly ahead of the other. The hands change places as the forward hand is brought toward the chest, and the other hand passes over it, exchanging places with it. It is not important which hand begins in front of the other or which hand passes over or under the other. The important thing is that they exchange places. X hands may be used instead of F hands. The sign can be executed directionally as a dual, left to right and right to left, to indicate that two people traded or exchanged something.

AGO, PAST

The open hand, palm facing back, is moved back over the shoulder. This is the temporal adverb which establishes the PAST TENSE as in effect for the following discourse until it is changed. The sign may be modified to indicate the recent past, RECENTLY, (scrunched shoulders, index finger handshape wiggled near the cheek) and the remote past, LONG AGO, (open shoulders, expansive movement, perhaps with both hands rolled back over the shoulder alternately).

FIT, MESH

The curved 5 hands are held with the palms toward the body, and they are brought together at the midline in neutral space so that the fingers MESH together. Bumped together twice the sign is ROOMMATE.

FORGET

The palm of the hand is brushed across the forehead, ending in the A handshape at the side of the forehead. The sign is related to KNOW, which taps the fingers of the open hand on the forehead. An alternative more emphatic sign for FORGET strokes the tip of the middle finger of the OPEN 8 hand across the forehead, implying BLANK MIND.

ENOUGH

The nondominant fist or O hand is held in neutral space with the opening of the O hand facing up. The palm of the dominant hand is brushed outward across the top of the nondominant hand as it moves forward from the body. The sign may be executed as a single, emphatic movement or in several brief reduplicated movements.

DO, ACT, BEHAVE

The C hands, palms down, are moved back and forth in a parallel motion in neutral space. If they are moved back and forth alternately in opposite directions, the sign is WORK, BUSY. This sign does not translate the English auxiliary verb, *do, did.*

TEACH

The BABY O hands are held in a slightly elevated position in neutral space, and they are moved forward repeatedly. The sign may be motivated by the notion of taking something from the head and presenting it to someone else. The compound, TEACH + AGENT is TEACHER.

BEGIN, START

The index finger of the dominant hand is thrust between the index and middle fingers of the nondominant hand and twisted slightly, usually in a clockwise direction, but the opposite direction is also allowed.

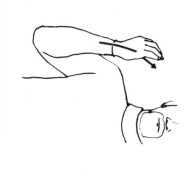

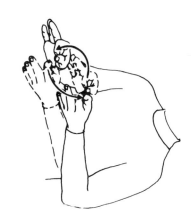

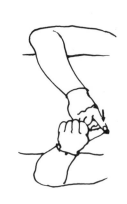

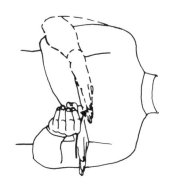

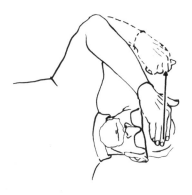

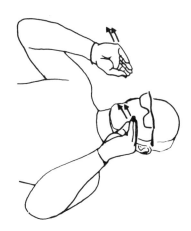

FLOWER 125

The clustered fingertips of the **BABY O** hands are touched to the upper lip under the nostrils. The sign imitates the smelling of a flower. An alternate execution gently opens the clustered fingers of the **BABY O** hand in front of the nose. An alternative sign holds an imaginary bouquet of flowers in the right fist and brings them to the nose as if to smell them.

PAY 126

The nondominant hand is held, palm up, in neutral space, and the index fingertip of the dominant hand is stroked outward across the other palm. If the index fingertip is jabbed into the other palm, the sign is DEBT. The sign can be executed directionally as the index fingertip is placed in the other palm and both hands are moved toward the listener for OWE YOU or toward the speaker for OWE ME.

COLLEGE 127

The palms are brought into contact, one hand above the other, in neutral space, and the upper hand is then raised above the other in a spiral movement. The sign is derived from SCHOOL, signed by clapping the hands together as if calling pupils to attention. In COLLEGE the elevated hand implies a school of higher education. For UNIVERSITY the elevated hand presents a U handshape as it completes its spiral.

COFFEE 128

The dominant fist makes a circular motion in a horizontal plane above the nondominant fist. The sign is derived from old fashioned coffee grinders, which turned a crank in a horizontal plane above a grinder, which allowed the grounds to be removed from a drawer in the base. The dominant fist is often in contact with the left fist as the sign is executed.

FARM 129

The thumb of the right 5 hand is stroked from left to right across the bottom of the chin. FARM + AGENT is FARMER. An alternative sign runs the little finger edge of the right B across the left palm, imitating a plow share plowing a field.

STEAL 130

The nondominant forearm is held in a horizontal plane across the body, and the dominant V hand is extended under the other arm and then drawn back to the body as the fingers close in a **BENT V** handshape.

VOLUNTEER, APPLY, CANDIDATE 131

The thumb and index finger of the dominant F hand grasp the shirt front near the shoulder and tug forward slightly. The sign implies that the person is pulling himself or herself into prominence by being a CANDIDATE for office, APPLYING for a position, or VOLUNTEERING for service.

MULTIPLY, FIGURE 132

The V hands, palms facing the speaker, are brought together several times so that the wrists are crossed repeatedly in front of the body. The sign refers primarily to the arithmetic operation of multiplication or to mathematical figuring.

DEPEND 133

The nondominant index finger is held in a horizontal plane in neutral space, and the dominant index finger is hooked over it as if hanging from it. If the movement of the dominant index finger is to hook the other index finger from underneath and lift it upward, the sign is SUSPEND.

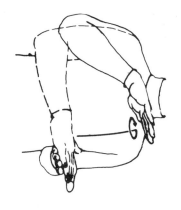 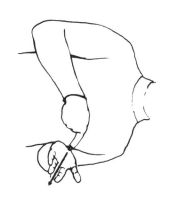 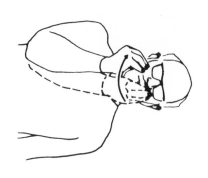

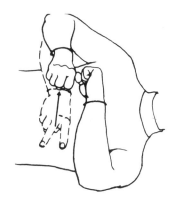  

 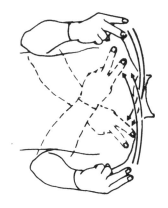 

134 IDEA

The extended little finger is held near the forehead with the palm facing the forehead, and it is brought upward and outward in a small arc. In an alternative execution the wrist is twisted as the sign, IDEA, is executed, so that the final position presents the palm facing outward. For the verb, IMAGINE, the movement is more elaborate: it consists of a series of small arcs or small circles as the I hand moves upward from the forehead.

135 BIRTH

The two hands are held close to the front of the body, palms up, and they are brought forward in an arc as if bringing something forward from the body. An alternative sign holds the nondominant arm, palm down, horizontally across the body, and the dominant hand, palm down, is brought down between the arm and the body and then forward out from the body. Either of these signs for BIRTH can form a compound with DAY to yield BIRTHDAY.

136 INSTITUTION, RESIDENTIAL SCHOOL FOR THE DEAF

The fist of the dominant I hand is struck twice against the top of the fist of the nondominant I hand or against the back of the nondominant fist. The dominant I hand may make a small circle before making contact with the other hand. The sign is related to the verb, ESTABLISH, executed with the thumb up A hand, CHURCH, executed with the C hand, and TEMPLE, executed with the T hand.

137 WE

The right index fingertip is touched to the right and then the left shoulder. The finger may be pointing upward, or it may be turned so that it points downward. US is signed similarly, but with the right U hand. If these signs are executed left handed, the shoulder positions are reversed.

138 FOOLISH, SILLY

The right Y hand, palm facing left, is waved back and forth in front of the forehead. The sign may be executed with a slight downward movement so as to brush the tip of the nose. A single forceful move across the face is FOOL.

139 MEAN, CRUEL, RUIN

Both hands are held in neutral space, with the fingers spread and bent, and with the palms facing, except that the dominant hand is closer to the speaker's body than the nondominant hand. Both hands are clenched into fists as the dominant hand moves forward and downward, scraping the knuckles of both hands against each other as it passes. The sign is generally accompanied by an appropriately cruel or mean facial expression.

140 WONDERFUL

Both hands are presented palms out in a forward movement that ends forcefully with a full stop. The sign is an adjective, and may occur as a predicate adjective (THAT WONDERFUL) or as modifying a noun (SHE WONDERFUL TEACHER).

141 WOOD, SAW

The nondominant hand is held palm down in neutral space, and the dominant hand, representing the blade of a hand saw, makes sawing motions across the back of the other hand. The sign is used metaphorically for SNORE.

142 HERE

The two hands, palms up, make tight circles in opposite directions in a horizontal plane in neutral space. Accompanied by a questioning facial expression, the sign is the interrogative adverb, WHERE? The locative, HERE, may also be indicated by pointing downward to a location near the speaker.

  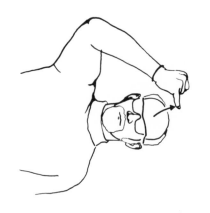

  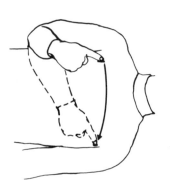

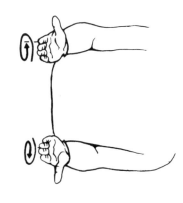  

ROAD, PATH 143

Both hands, palms facing and fingers pointing downward, trace a winding path forward from the body. For WAY, STREET the hands move forward in straight, parallel lines. WATER + PATH = RIVER, STREAM.

ANGRY, CROSS, MEAN 144

The 5 hand is held in front of the face, and it is curled inward as a CLAW hand with repeated internal movement of the fingers. Depending on nonmanual signals, the sign can span a wide range of nuances, from peeved to outraged. An alternative sign ANGRY jerks the CLAW hands, palms toward the body, upward toward the shoulders as if tearing at the skin.

UNTIL 145

The nondominant index finger is held with the tip pointing upward, and the dominant hand, index finger extended, is brought up in an arc and then downward to touch the tip of the other index finger. This sign is distinguished from the preposition, TO, in that the latter brings the dominant index fingertip directly toward the other index fingertip to make contact with it, whereas UNTIL brings the dominant index finger toward the other in an upward arc.

LEAD 146

The nondominant hand is held with the thumb edge up and the fingers pointing forward. The dominant fist grasps the tips of the fingers of the nondominant hand and pulls the hand forward from the body. LEAD + AGENT = LEADER. If the pulling movement of the dominant hand is off to the side in an erratic path, the sign is LEAD ASTRAY.

DECIDE 147

Both open hands are held up near the face with palms facing, the dominant hand near the forehead. Both hands are then brought down forcibly to a full stop, ending with F hands, palms facing, in neutral space. The sign may be a compound derived from THINK + a modified execution of JUDGE. The verb, JUDGE, moves both F hands, palms facing, alternately up and down in neutral space. The noun, JUDGE, is executed as a compound, JUDGE + AGENT.

PITY 148

The middle fingertip is stroked briefly on the chest near the heart, and it is then extended outward toward the imaginary object and stroked one or two times. The first element of the sign is sometimes deleted. The second element is sometimes executed as a small circle in a vertical plane. In religious contexts a two-handed version of this sign is sometimes used for MERCY or HAVE MERCY. The sign can be made a reflexive, SELF PITY, by directing the second element of the compound toward the speaker's own body.

TRY, ATTEMPT 149

The fists or the T hands, palms facing, are moved forward from the body with tensed muscles to indicate an expenditure of effort. In some regions, the sign is executed with A hands, thumbs up, stroked downward from both shoulders.

TREE 150

The elbow of the dominant forearm is rested in the nondominant palm, and the 5 hand of the dominant hand is agitated, representing the movement of leaves on a tree. If both arms are moved horizontally as the sign is executed, it represents TREES or FOREST.

CONVERSE, CONVERSATION 151

Both hands are held in front of the face, index fingers near the mouth and pointing upward, one hand slightly ahead of the other. The index fingers are moved alternately back and forth by bending the wrists. If both index fingers are moved forward in unison by bending both wrists, the sign is ANSWER. A one-handed execution is ORDER, as from a menu, or COMMAND.

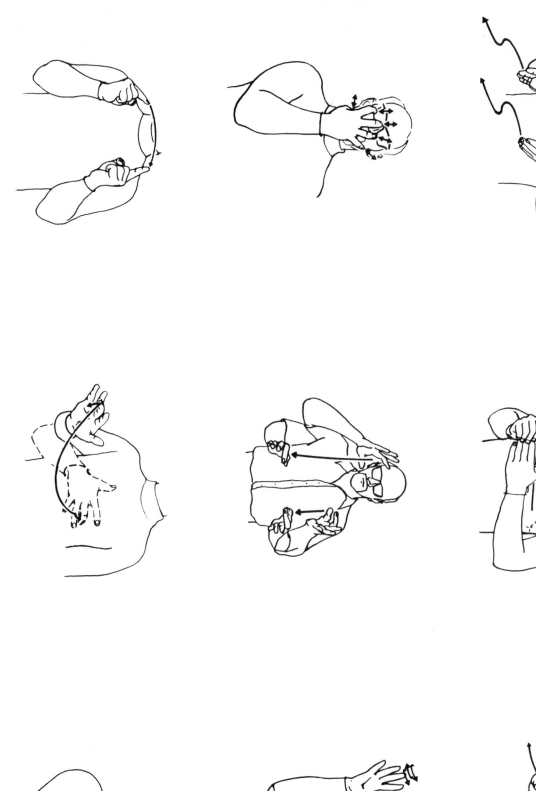
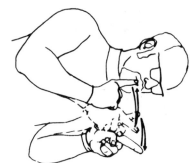

152 BEAUTIFUL

The right 5 hand, palm toward the face, begins at the right cheek and makes a counterclockwise circle, ending with the thumb and fingers clustered together at the chin. A more emphatic execution completes the circle and then ends with the fingers clustered together off to the right of the face. A left-handed execution makes a clockwise circle.

153 EXAGGERATE, PROLONG

The dominant S hand is touched against the nondominant S hand in such a way that the fists are lined up end to end in neutral space. The dominant hand is then moved forward from the body, away from the other hand, with a marked wavy motion. If the dominant fist is bumped against the edge non-dominant fist repeatedly, the sign is ADVERTISE, PUBLICIZE, PUBLICITY.

154 HOUSE

The fingertips of both open hands are touched together in neutral space, and the hands are brought out and down, tracing the roof and sides of a house. In casual usage the movement may be limited to tracing the outline of a roof. Executed with V hands, the sign is TENT. If the fingertips are touched together two or more times as both hands are moved horizontally in neutral space, the sign is TOWN, CITY.

155 NONE OF MY BUSINESS, I AM NOT RESPONSIBLE

The middle fingertips of both hands flick imaginary objects off opposite shoulders. A one-handed execution is also permissible. Nonmanual clues indicate whether the sign simply disclaims responsibility or whether it is a refusal to have anything to do with the matter. An alternative execution flicks off the shoulders on the same sides, without crossing the arms.

156 PREACH

The F hand, palm facing outward with the fingers pointing up, is moved forward briefly two or more times in front of the shoulder. A related sign, LECTURE, is executed with the open hand, palm to the side. PREACH + AGENT = PREACHER.

157 TEA

The nondominant O hand is held with the opening at the top, representing a cup, and the pinched thumb and index finger of the dominant hand make small circular movements at the opening. The sign is said to represent stirring a tea bag in a cup of water.

158 EACH

The dominant A hand, thumb up, is stroked down along the back of the thumb of the nondominant A hand, thumb up. If the downward movement occurs two or more times, the sign is EVERY. These signs may be executed in the direction of their referent or a location that represents the referent.

159 BUILD, BUILDING

The fingertips of the BENT B hands are placed on top of the fingers of the other BENT B hand, alternating the placement as both hands move upward in neutral space. The sign may imitate laying bricks. The sign may be executed with the extended index and middle fingers of the H hands.

160 LAY OFF, LAID OFF

The nondominant hand is held, palm up, in neutral space. The fingertips of the dominant hand are placed in contact with the little finger side of the other palm. The dominant hand is, then, brushed outward and away from the other palm. The sign refers specifically to a dismissal from work that is different from being horizontal from being fired.

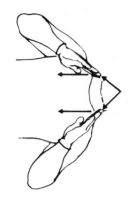  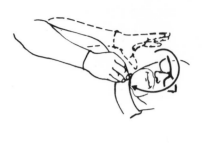

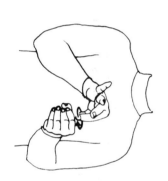  

161 RIGHT

The right R hand is moved off to the RIGHT in neutral space. For LEFT the right or left L hand is moved off to the LEFT in neutral space. This sign does not translate *morally right* or *right* in the sense of *correct*. The points of the compass, NORTH, EAST, SOUTH, and WEST, are executed with initialized signs moved up, right, down, and left, respectively.

162 SOUR

The index finger is pointed to the side of the mouth, and it makes a twisting motion at the right side of the mouth or chin. A related sign, BITTER, jabs the index finger sharply toward the mouth as the lips are pinched together, as if tasting something BITTER. Executed without the lip sign, the tip of the index finger touched to the mouth or chin is the sign DISAPPOINTED.

163 NEAR

The BENT B hands are held with the palms toward the body, the nondominant hand in neutral space and the dominant hand either farther away from the body or closer to the body than the nondominant hand. The dominant hand is then moved close to the nondominant hand. The nondominant hand provides a frame of reference, and the meaning, NEAR, is represented by the relation of the dominant hand to the nondominant hand in the final position of the sign. The difference in the two executions reflects a difference in whether the proximity represented by NEAR is also near the speaker or whether it is near some other point in space. NEAR + AGENT = NEIGHBOR. The sign may also be executed as a verb, COME NEAR, APPROACH.

164 BUT, DIFFERENT, ON THE CONTRARY

The crossed index fingers, palms facing outward, are pulled apart. The sign is an adversative conjunction, BUT, ON THE CONTRARY; however, it is not used in exactly the same manner and contexts as the English *but*. Nonmanual signals often serve as juncture markers in ASL, with the result that specific signs, like BUT, are unnecessary. Moreover, the sign glossed BUT may also be used as a descriptive adjective, DIFFERENT.

165 HUNGRY, WISH, LONG FOR

The fingertips and thumb of the dominant C hand are drawn down the center of the chest. The underlying metaphor may be a hollow tube for a stomach, implying an empty, hungry stomach. The sign is used metaphorically for LONG FOR, WISH.

166 LATE, TARDY

The dominant hand is held hear the waist with the fingers pointing downward and the palm facing backward. The hand is moved backward behind the body with a bending of the wrist. A reduplicated execution is the sign NOT YET. A forceful gesture backwards at the waist is VERY LATE.

167 VACATION

The thumbs of both 5 hands are touched to the shoulders two or more times. If the thumbs are placed in contact with the shoulders as the fingers are wiggled, the sign is LOAF.

168 THROUGH

The nondominant hand is held in neutral space with the palm facing the other hand. The dominant hand, palm up, is thrust through the middle and fourth fingers of the nondominant hand. The sign is generally used for the preposition, THROUGH, but it may also serve as a verb, GO THROUGH. The nondominant hand provides a frame of reference, and the movement of the dominant hand is THROUGH the nondominant hand.

169 INDIFFERENT, NEVERTHELESS, ANYWAY, DON'T CARE

The nondominant BENT B hand is held palm up in neutral space with the fingers pointing upward. The dominant hand slaps the raised fingers back and forth. The facial expression may also imply indifference. Other English translations that may serve are *It doesn't matter, in any case,* or *it makes no difference.*

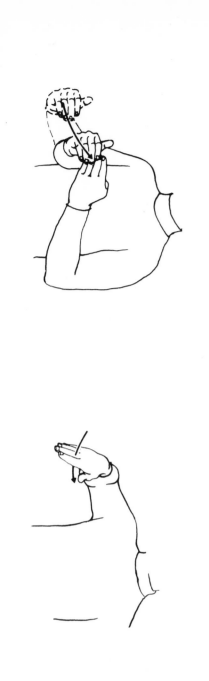
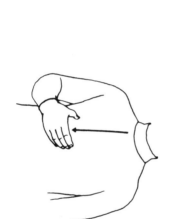

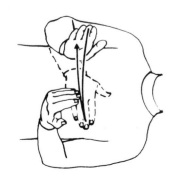
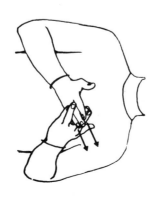
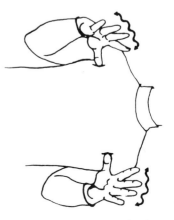

170 GOD

The right hand, palm to the left, is raised above eye level in an upward gesture with a slight twist of the wrist. The hand may make a small arc toward the head as the sign is executed. A respectful expression generally accompanies the sign, and the eyes may glance upward as the sign is executed. The raised index finger is sometimes used to refer to GOD.

171 UGLY

Both hands are crossed in front of the face with the index fingers extended and the palms facing downward. The hands are drawn across the face in opposite directions, uncrossing the arms, at the same time as the index fingers are curled into X hands. The sign may be motivated by the notion of facial disfigurement. It may be executed with one hand.

172 SAVE, CONSERVE

The nondominant fist is held in front of the body with the fingers toward the body. The dominant V hand, palm toward the body, is placed against the back of the nondominant fist. The sign does not translate *save* in the sense of *free*, *liberate*.

173 FORK

The fingertips of the dominant V hand are touched into the nondominant palm. The V hand is twisted slightly, and the fingertips are touched into the palm a second time. The dominant V hand can serve as a classifier for a FORK, and, stuck into the back of the nondominant fist, serve as the sign POTATO, and, stuck against the palm and then the back of the nondominant hand, serve as the sign TOAST.

174 HAPPEN

The extended index fingers, palms up, are held in neutral space, and the hands are turned over quickly with a twist of both wrists. If the hands are moved forward as the sign is executed, it is DURING, WHILE. If the sign begins over the right shoulder and ends in neutral space, it is UNTIL NOW, SINCE, ALL ALONG, FOR A DURATION OF TIME.

175 MISS

The dominant C hand is moved quickly across the face, ending as a closed fist. The movement resembles an attempt to catch a flying insect. A related sign executed across the forehead with a thoughtful facial expression is GUESS.

176 TOILET

The dominant T hand is waved back and forth or moved in a tight counterclockwise circle in front of the shoulder. An alternative sign is the fingerspelled sign R-R for RESTROOM.

177 DEFEND, GUARD

The nondominant forearm is held in a horizontal plane in neutral space, and the dominant forearm, also horizontal, is moved in front of it as if holding a shield. An alternative execution braces both arms in a defensive posture, bringing them to a full stop, as if warding off danger.

178 HOW?

The nondominant hand is held with the palm toward the body, and the index finger edge of the dominant hand is brought into contact with the nondominant hand as both hands are brought forward with twists of the wrists, ending with the palms up in neutral space. In an alternate version the backs of the fingers of both curved hands, thumbs up, are brought into contact in neutral space, and both hands are rolled up toward the body and out, ending with the palms up.

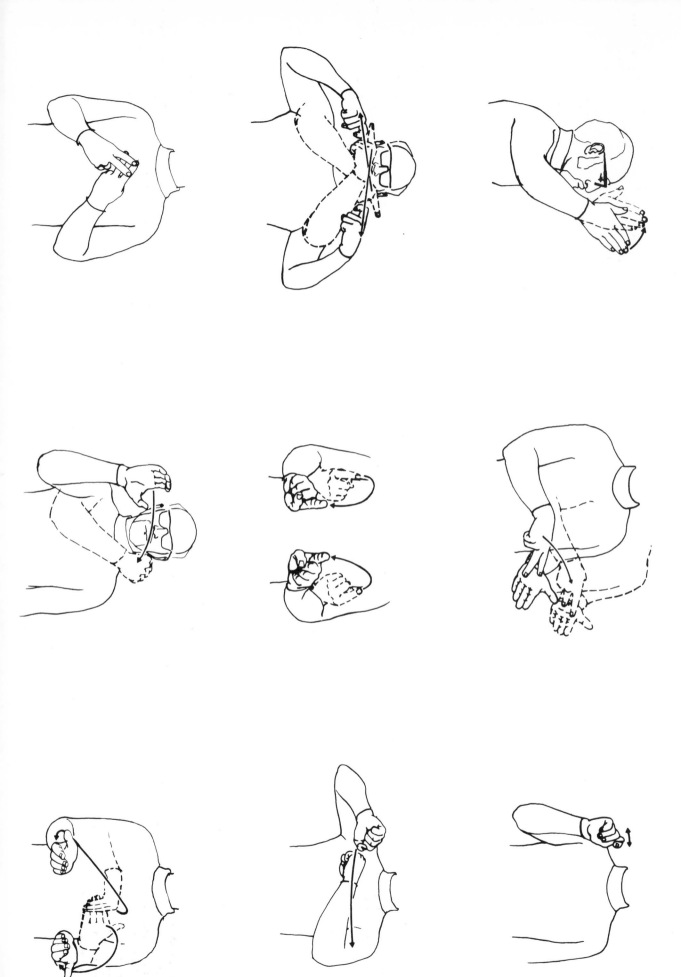

179 — ONLY, ALONE

The raised index finger, palm out, is turned so that the palm is toward the speaker's face, and the index finger is then moved forward in neutral space, presenting the numeral, ONE. An alternative execution presents the numeral ONE with the palm toward the speaker's face and slowly traces a small counterclockwise circle.

180 — WHEN?

The nondominant index finger is extended, and the dominant index finger makes a clockwise circle near the other fingertip and then touches it. This sign is generally an interrogative adverb, but it may also be used as a relative adverb like the English, *when*.

181 — DREAM

The tip of the index finger is placed near the forehead, and the finger is wiggled as the hand moves up and away from the forehead. A related sign, IMAGINE, traces little circles with the I hand as it moves up and away from the forehead.

182 — LAZY

The palm or thumb of the L hand is tapped against the opposite shoulder. A related sign, LOAF, touches the thumb of both 5 hands against the shoulders and wiggles the fingers. If the thumbs of the 5 hands are tapped against the shoulders, the sign is VACATION.

183 — HUH? WHAT? WHERE? WHO?

The index finger is pointed upward, palm out, and wagged back and forth with a questioning facial expression. The sign can stand for almost any kind of question, depending on the situation or context.

184 — FOLLOW

The nondominant A hand, thumb up, is held in neutral space some distance from the body, and the dominant A hand, thumb up, moves behind it as both hands move forward from the body. The handshapes represent the nouns, and the movement serves as a verb of motion. FOLLOW + AGENT = FOLLOWER, DISCIPLE. CHASE makes small circles with the dominant hand as it follows, sometimes gaining on the non-dominant hand. AVOID moves the dominant hand in an evasive action behind the other hand. ACCOMPANY moves both hands forward side by side. PASS passes the nondominant hand with the dominant hand. For LAG BEHIND the dominant hand is drawn back from the other hand, sometimes with a waving movement of the raised thumb.

184

185 — ONE ANOTHER, EACH OTHER, ASSOCIATE

The A hands are held so that the thumb of the nondominant hand is pointing upward and the thumb of the dominant hand is pointing downward. The thumbs then make counterclockwise circles around each other as both hands move in a large counterclockwise circle in a horizontal plane in neutral space. The sign serves as the indefinite pronoun, EACH OTHER, ONE ANOTHER, and as the verb, ASSOCIATE. A related sign executed with the two 4 hands is MINGLE, SOCIALIZE.

186 — HEAVEN

The back of the dominant hand rests in the nondominant palm in neutral space. The hands are brought apart and upward in front of the face, the hands are turned over, so that their palms are down, and the dominant hand is moved under the other palm as if entering the space beyond it. In an alternate version, the hands are held above the head, palms down, and they trace an arch as they are brought downward, depicting the vault of the HEAVENS or SKY.

187 — TIME, O'CLOCK

The index finger points to the top of the opposite wrist, where a watch is likely to be worn. To indicate TIME on a clock, the sign TIME is executed first and then the numeral. For example, for *four o'clock* one would sign TIME FOUR rather than FOUR TIME, since the latter might be construed to mean *four times*.

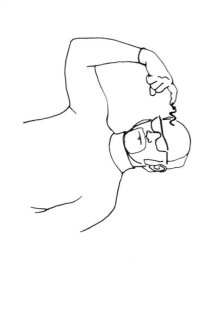  

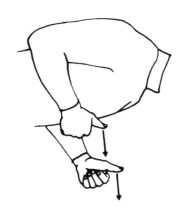 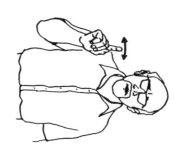 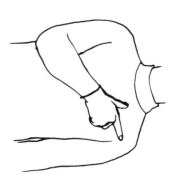

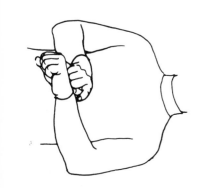 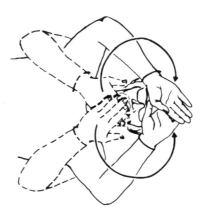 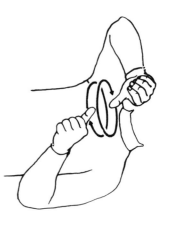

188

STAND

The nondominant hand is held, palm up, in neutral space, and the inverted dominant **V** hand is placed so as to STAND on the nondominant palm. The nondominant palm serves as the base for other related signs in which the inverted **V** hand imitates the action or position of the legs of a person, *e.g.*, DANCE, JUMP, FALL, LIE DOWN, and KNEEL.

189

PLEASANT, COOL

Both hands are held with the palms facing backward near the cheeks with the fingers pointing upward. The palms are bent several times as if fanning the cheeks with air or the fingers are wiggled as if feeling the cool breeze filter through the fingers. The sign is generally used to refer to PLEASANT weather, but it may also be used to describe a PLEASANT feeling.

190

SATISFIED

The edges of both hands, palms down, are placed against the chest with the dominant hand above the nondominant hand. The hands may make a slight downward movement just as they come into contact with the chest. A more informal, colloquial sign for FULL, SATISFIED brings the back of the hand, palm down, up under the chin, pressing it against the underside of the chin.

191

PRACTICE

The nondominant index finger is extended, and the knuckles of the dominant **A** hand are brushed against the edge of the index finger as the **A** hand is moved briskly back and forth.

192

I, ME

The dominant index finger is pointed to the speaker's chest. The execution is the same whether the pronoun is the subject, I, or the object, ME. If the index finger points to the listener, the sign is YOU. Directed elsewhere it can refer to HE, SHE, IT, HIM, HER, YOU (pl.), THEY, or THEM. WE is somewhat more complex: the index finger is touched to the right and then the left shoulder (the opposite sequence for left-handed speakers). The **W** handshape may be used. Similarly, US touches the right **U** hand to the right and left shoulders (opposite for left-handed speakers). There is an initialized sign, I, which touches the **I** hand against the chest.

193

TAKE UP, UNDERTAKE

The **5** hands are held, palms down, in neutral space. They are brought upward in space as they close into **A** hands. The action imitates lifting something up and holding on to it. The sign can be reversed as DROP, DISCONTINUE WORK.

194

NATION

The nondominant fist is held, palm down, in neutral space. The dominant **N** hand makes a small circle above the other hand and is brought down so as to make contact with the back of the other fist or wrist. The sign translates *country* in the sense of *nation*. This same execution in some contexts is the sign NATURAL, or NATURALLY. There is another sign for COUNTRY in the sense of COUNTRYSIDE, FARM COUNTRY: the dominant palm or **Y** hand makes a small circle on the outside of the nondominant forearm near the elbow. This sign may be motivated by the leather patches worn on a jacket by gentlemen who live in the country.

195

BLOOD

The nondominant hand is held in neutral space with the palm toward the body. The dominant **5** hand references the region of the mouth and then is brought downward over the nondominant hand as the fingers make a fluttering motion. The sign represents something red flowing over the back of the nondominant hand. A similar fluttering motion of the fingers of the **5** hand is used for the sign SWEAT, PERSPIRE, which moves the right **5** hand from right to left across the forehead as the fingers are fluttered (the opposite movement for left-handed speakers).

196

SORRY, SORROW

The dominant fist is rubbed in a clockwise, circular movement over the heart. This is the sign typically used to say, *I am sorry*. Other signs executed over the heart involving emotions include GRIEF (the fists are clenched as the wrists are twisted, rubbing the fists together), CONSCIENCE (the extended index finger is struck against the chest), and love (the fists are clenched and the wrists are crossed over the heart).

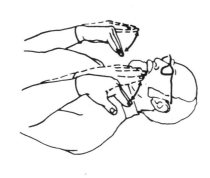

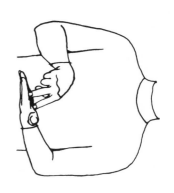

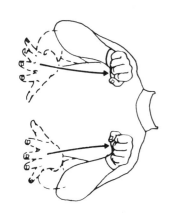

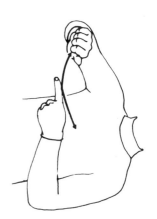

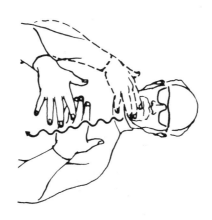

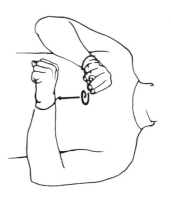

PROTESTANT

The nondominant hand is held, palm up, in neutral space, and the dominant **BENT V** hand is placed in the other palm so as to represent a kneeling position.

PROMISE, SWEAR

The dominant index finger or the tips of the fingers of the dominant hand are brought near the mouth, and the palm of the dominant hand is then struck against the opening formed by the top of the nondominant fist, palm to the side. An alternative execution brings the right hand near the mouth and then raises it in the air in a gesture similar to taking an oath in a courtroom.

WAR

The **5** hands, palms toward each other, are moved back and forth in front of the body, representing the advancing and retreating forces at the front lines. A similar execution with extended index fingers is STRUGGLE, STRIVE.

TIGER

The fingers of the **5** hands trace stripes on both cheeks as the hands are drawn apart at the face. Many signs for animals depict a salient feature of the animal: the long neck for GIRAFFE, the trunk for ELEPHANT, horns for DEER, the white stripe for SKUNK, *etc.*

HOSPITAL

The dominant **H** hand traces a cross on the opposite shoulder or upper arm, representing the patch or insignia worn by hospital personnel. Executed with the **P** hand, the sign is PATIENT.

NEXT

The nondominant hand is held with the palm toward the body, fingers pointed to the side. The dominant hand is held similarly, but closer to the body. The dominant hand is then moved up and over the index finger edge of the nondominant hand, ending with the palm near the back of the other hand's fingers. If both hands make this movement alternately as the hands move forward in neutral space, the sign is ADVANCE, PROGRESS.

BELIEVE

The dominant hand is brought near the forehead, referencing the region associated with mental signs, and then both hands are clasped together in neutral space. An alternative sign, TRUST, is executed similarly, except that the second element clenches both fists with the one fist slightly above the other.

COME

The index fingers of both hands are rolled over one another as they are brought toward the body. In another version both index fingers are brought toward the body simultaneously in an arc. One hand only may be used. The reverse of these executions is GO. A natural beckoning gesture may also be used for COME.

USE

The **U** hand in an upright position, palm facing out, makes a small circle above the back of the nondominant fist. Alternatively, the U hand may be bumped against the back of the nondominant fist several times.

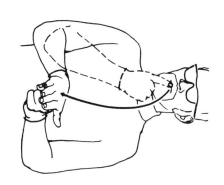

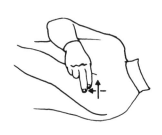
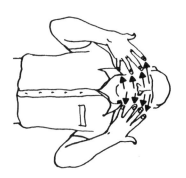

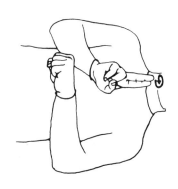

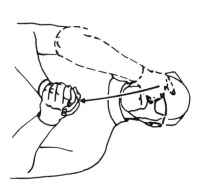

206

SIT

The extended fingers of the **H** hand, palm down, are brought down and placed across the backs of the fingers of the nondominant **H** hand, palm down. The fingers of the dominant **H** hand may be bent like legs dangling over the edge of the other extended fingers. The verb, SIT, is executed as a single, smooth movement. The noun, CHAIR, is a tense reduplicated execution in neutral space. The verb, SIT, may also be executed as a natural gesture, slouching in neutral space as the hands or arms are crossed in a relaxed position.

207

SURPRISE, SURPRISED

The tips of the thumbs and index fingers are touched together, and the hands are held at the sides of the face near the eye. The thumbs and index fingers are spread apart quickly, indicating the widening of the eyes when one is SURPRISED. A related sign, AWAKEN, is signed similarly, but the fingers are spread apart slowly, and the eyes may open as the sign is executed.

208

READ

The nondominant palm is held, palm up, in neutral space, and the fingertips of the dominant **V** hand move down the palm or left to right on the palm as if following lines of type.

209

ACROSS, AFTER

The nondominant hand is held, palm down, in neutral space, and the dominant hand, palm to the side, is stroked ACROSS the back of the other hand. In some contexts this sign can mean AFTER. The sign can also be used as a verb: CROSS, GO ACROSS.

210

MAKE

The fists are held in neutral space, the dominant hand above the nondominant hand. They are bumped against each other as the wrists are twisted back and forth in opposite directions. If the fists are rubbed against each other as the wrists are twisted, the sign is FIX, REPAIR.

211

QUIT

The nondominant hand forms an **O** in neutral space, and the extended fingers of the dominant **V** hand, are brought forcefully out from the grasp of the other hand. The opposite action is JOIN, PARTICIPATE.

212

NEW

The nondominant hand is held, palm up, in neutral space, and the back of the dominant hand, palm up, is brushed against the other palm as it moves across it. For right handed speakers, the movement is from right to left across the hand, placed in the opening of the **O**

213

CHURCH

The dominant **C** hand is placed on the back of the nondominant fist. Executed with the **T** hand, the sign is TEMPLE.

214

FINISH, DONE, ALREADY

The two **5** hands, palms up or palms facing, are turned over quickly with a twist of both wrists. The sign is used for an action completed in the past. For example, FINISH EAT would be translated, *I have eaten.* FINISH followed by an independent clause is also used after a durative, as in WORK WORK WORK FINISH REST *When I had finished doing a lot of work, I rested.*

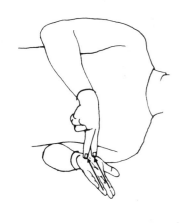 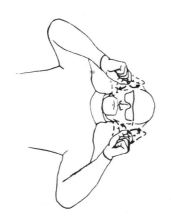 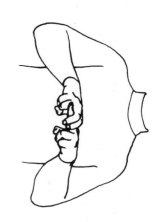

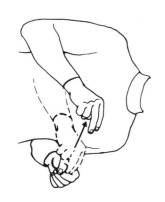  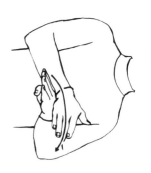

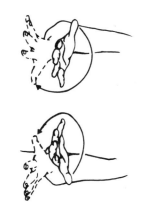 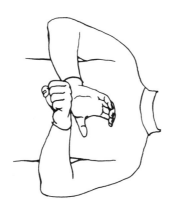 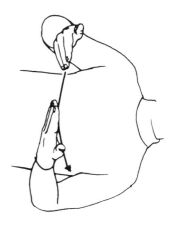

WEIGH, WEIGHT, POUNDS 215

The nondominant index finger is extended horizontally in neutral space, representing the beam of a balance scale. The dominant index finger is placed across the other index finger and rocked slightly, imitating the movement of a scale that is almost in balance. The sign may be executed using the extended fingers of the two **H** hands.

STORY 216

The thumbs and index fingers of the **F** or **G** hands are interlocked and drawn apart two or more times as the hands make small circles in neutral space. The wrists may be twisted so that the contact is made first with the right hand above the left and then the left hand above the right. The sign may be executed with **BABY O** handshapes. The verb, TELL A STORY, requires a larger circular movement by the hands between contacts, and fewer reduplications. A related sign, SENTENCE, touches the thumbs and index fingers of the **F** hands together in neutral space and then draws the two hands apart horizontally in either a straight or a wavy motion. Initialized with **L** hands this sign is LANGUAGE.

LEARN 217

The nondominant hand is held, palm up, in neutral space. The fingertips of the dominant **5** hand are brushed against the surface of the palm and then brought together in a cluster as they move toward the forehead. The sign represents taking something from the hand and placing it in the head. LEARN + AGENT = STUDENT.

ACCEPT 218

The two **5** hands are held, palms down, in neutral space, and they are brought into contact with the chest as they close into **BABY O** handshapes. Nonverbal clues typically indicate whether the acceptance is willing or unwilling. The sign is used to acknowledge assent. For example, I ACCEPT could be translated *I did what he said.* The sign may be executed with only one hand.

COW 219

The thumb of the **Y** hand is touched to the side of the forehead and the hand is rocked forward one or more times with a twist of the wrist. An alternative sign brings the **Y** hand out from the forehead in an arc, tracing the outline of the horn of a longhorn steer. Related signs are HORSE, executed with the raised index and middle finger at the side of the forehead, DEER, executed with the thumb of the **5** hand touched to the side of the forehead, and MULE, executed with the edge of the **B** hand touched to the side of the forehead and bent forward one or more times.

COUSIN 220

The **C** hand is rocked at the side of the head with a twist of the wrist. This sign may be executed near the temple to represent a male cousin and near the jaw to represent a female cousin, but the sign is usually executed at the side of the head, leaving gender ambiguous. NEPHEW and NIECE are signed with the **N** hand rocked at the temple and jaw, respectively, acknowledging the gender regions for these signs.

ARRIVE 221

The nondominant hand is held, palm up, in neutral space, and the dominant hand, palm up, is brought forward and then down into the other palm as both hands move forward from the body.

JEW, JEWISH 222

The **B** hand is brought downward from the chin as if following the length of a beard, ending in a **BABY O** handshape. In formal circumstances the sign may be executed with two hands. A casual execution strokes the fingertips of the **BENT 5** hand on the chin one or more times. Nonmanual features accompanying the execution may imply a racial slur.

MEET 223

The two hands, palms facing and index fingers pointing upward, are brought toward each other in neutral space. The raised index fingers are classifiers representing two people, and the movement of the fingers implies a meeting. A variety of verbs of motion may be constructed from the movement of one or both raised index fingers. If several people are to MEET, the **5** hands are held in neutral space with the palms facing each other, and they are brought together as the fingers are clustered together. A reduplicated execution with the hands held close together is the noun, MEETING.

 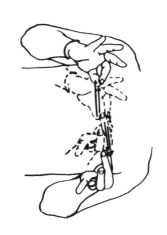 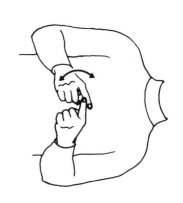

 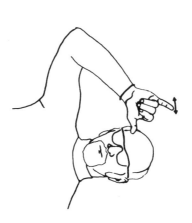 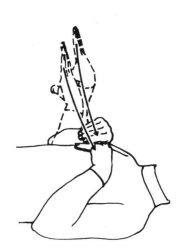

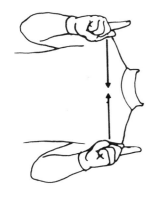 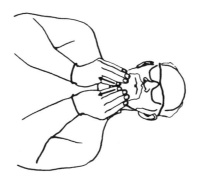 

224 LISTEN, HEAR, EAR

The index finger points to the ear for the noun, EAR. For the verb, LISTEN, HEAR, the facial expression adds an attentive pose.

225 FULL

The nondominant O hand is held with the palm to the side and the opening at the top. The dominant hand, palm down, is scraped across the opening as it moves toward the body. The dominant hand may make a slight arc as it moves over the other hand, implying that it is full to the brim.

226 THINK, THOUGHT

The index fingertip is touched to the forehead or it makes a small circle on the forehead. Other mental signs executed with the index finger on or near the forehead include DREAM (a waving movement up from the forehead), UNDERSTAND (flicked upward at the side of the forehead), and WISE (the curved index finger moved downward in front of the forehead).

227 VISIT

The two V hands, palms facing the speaker, make circles out from the body in an alternating motion.

228 MORNING

The nondominant forearm is held in a horizontal plane in neutral space, representing the horizon. The dominant forearm, palm up, is brought up from under the other forearm, representing the sun coming up over the horizon. If the execution involves a movement of the forearm up to nearly a vertical position, the sign is ALL MORNING. Placed on hand of the horizontal forearm in a vertical position, the sign is NOON. Rested on the forearm at an angle, it is AFTERNOON, representing the sun in the AFTERNOON sky. If this execution involves a movement through the space from NOON to LATE AFTERNOON, the sign is ALL AFTERNOON. If the wrist is placed against the horizontal forearm with a BENT B handshape, the sign is EVENING or NIGHT.

229 FUN

The fingertips of the nondominant H hand are extended horizontally in neutral space with the palm down. The fingertips of the dominant H hand are brought near the nose and then downward to strike against the top of the extended fingertips of the other H hand. The fingers are slapped against each other alternately as the hands move up and down in neutral space. The sign may be executed with only the second element of the compound. It is often executed as a fingerspelled sign, F-U-N. A related sign, FUNNY, brushes the fingertips of the H hand against the nose either once with a forceful movement or two or three times in an abbreviated movement.

230 CHOKED UP

The 5 hand is held near the throat with the palm toward the chest. It is brought up to the throat as it is clenched into a fist. The sign can be either CHOKED UP WITH ANGER or CHOKED UP WITH LAUGHTER, depending on the context. In addition to the context, the facial expression will indicate which of the alternative meanings is intended.

231 SHIP

The nondominant hand is held, palm up, in neutral space. The dominant hand assumes the handshape of the VEHICLE classifier, namely, the thumb up with the index and middle fingers pointing forward. The VEHICLE classifier is rested on the nondominant palm, and both hands are moved as if floating on waves. The sign may be executed without support from the nondominant palm.

232 ROCK

The back of the nondominant fist is struck by the back of the dominant fist or S hand. A related sign, HARD, strikes the back of the nondominant fist with the knuckle of the middle finger of the BENT V hand.

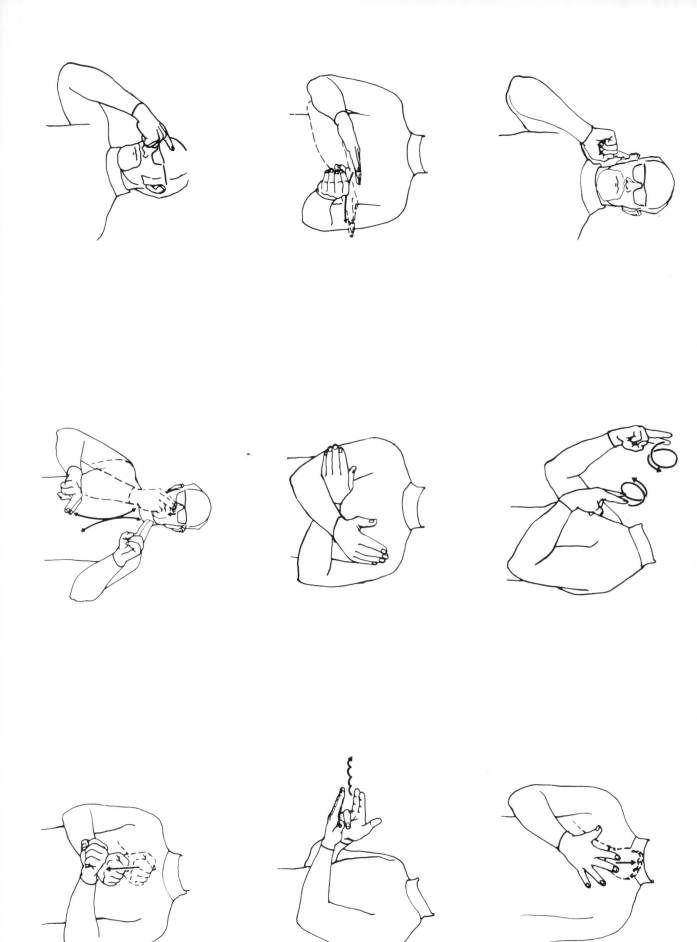

233 — BREAK

The fists are held in neutral space, palms down, as if holding a stick. They carry out the natural gesture of breaking the imaginary stick by twisting both wrists.

234 — TIME

The nondominant hand is held in neutral space with the fingers pointing upward and the palm to the side. The dominant T hand makes a clockwise circle on the palm, beginning at the 12:00 position. This is the sign TIME in a generic sense; clock time is signaled by pointing to the wrist where a watch is worn and then announcing the appropriate numeral. A related sign, HOUR, traces a circle on the nondominant palm with the dominant hand, index finger extended. The wrist may be twisted as this latter sign is executed so that the extended index finger points to the perimeter of the nondominant palm, which represents the face of a clock.

235 — MEET, MEETING

The 5 hands, palms facing, are brought together in neutral space as the fingertips are clustered together. This sign implies a MEETING of several people. Two upright index fingers are brought together in neutral space for a MEETING between two people.

236 — IGNORANT

The back of the dominant V hand is placed against the forehead. It is likely that an appropriate facial expression will be displayed as the sign is executed. A related sign, DUMB, STUPID, strikes the knuckles of the fist against the forehead.

237 — BOOK

The palms of both hands are placed together in neutral space and then opened. The sign depicts a book as its covers are opened.

238 — BOY, MAN, MALE

The thumb and fingers of the dominant hand are brought together in front of the forehead as if tipping a hat. The sign may occur alone for BOY or MAN, or it may be followed by a sign indicating SHORT or TALL stature. Followed by the sign FINE, it is GENTLEMAN. The sign occurs in a number of compounds, representing the male gender region, although the handshape of the second element of the compound often spreads to the first. Examples of compounds with the MALE gender region are BROTHER, HUSBAND, and SON.

239 — SMART, INTELLIGENT

The tip of the raised index finger is touched to the forehead, and the hand is then raised upward and outward from the head. An alternative sign, CLEVER, SMART, touches the tip of the middle finger of the OPEN 8 handshape to the forehead and then turns the palm quickly outward with a twist of the wrist.

240 — TO, TOWARD

The tip of the dominant extended index finger approaches and touches the tip of the extended nondominant index finger. This is a preposition, and its meaning is represented by the relation of the dominant hand to the nondominant hand.

241 — DIE, DEATH

The hands are held side by side in a horizontal plane in front of the body, the nondominant hand palm up and the dominant hand palm down. Both hands are turned over as they move slightly to the side. The sign DISAPPEAR, GONE is sometimes used for DIE: the nondominant hand is held in neutral space with the palm toward the body, and the dominant 5 hand, palm to the body, is brought down past the other hand as the fingers are clustered together.

 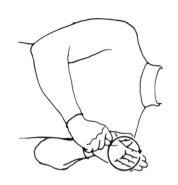 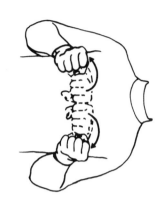

 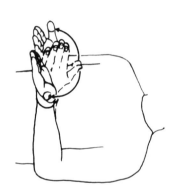 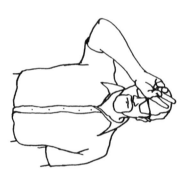

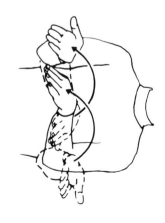  

242 IN, INSIDE

The fingers of the dominant BABY O or B hand are thrust into the opening formed by the nondominant O hand, held with the opening facing upward. The opposite execution is OUT. If the nondominant hand is held in a more relaxed handshape, palm downward, and the dominant hand, palm down, is thrust under and past it, the sign is the verb, ENTER, GO IN. The opposite execution is GO OUT.

243 WRONG

The fingers of the dominant Y hand are touched to the chin. The sign is used frequently with a wide range of nuances, from an honest MISTAKE to MORALLY WRONG.

244 TALL

The BENT B hand, palm down, is raised above eye level and brought to a full stop. The opposite sign, SMALL, brings the palm down to waist level to a full stop. Combined with a gender marker (MALE or FEMALE) the sign means ADULT MALE, ADULT FEMALE, LITTLE BOY, or LITTLE GIRL. An alternative sign TALL holds the nondominant hand, fingers pointing up and palm to the side, in neutral space, and the raised index finger on the dominant hand is scraped upward along the other palm.

245 HUSBAND

The dominant hand is brought near the forehead, referencing the MALE gender region, and the two hands are then clasped together in neutral space, as in the sign MARRY. WIFE is executed similarly, but with the first element of the compound referencing the FEMALE gender region.

246 THANK, THANKS, THANK YOU

The fingertips of both hands are brought near the mouth and then moved forward and outward from the face. One hand may be used. This is the common expression of gratitude corresponding to the English, *Thank you.*

247 SHOW

The nondominant palm is held with the palm facing out and the fingers pointing upward. The index fingertip of the dominant hand is placed in the center of the other palm, and both hands are shoved forward into neutral space. The sign may be executed directionally. An alternative execution taps the dominant index finger in the raised nondominant palm two or more times or simply points toward the palm.

248 MARRY

The two C hands, palms facing, are clasped together in neutral space. This sign is the second element of the compounds, HUSBAND (MALE + MARRY) and WIFE (FEMALE + MARRY). The dominant hand may make a small circle before the hands are joined together.

249 NOT

The dominant A hand is held, thumb up, under the chin, and the tip of the thumb is brushed under the chin as the thumb is brought forward in an arc. The sign is often accompanied by a negative head-shake.

250 DAY

The nondominant hand is held palm up in neutral space with the arm in a horizontal plane. The elbow of the dominant hand is rested on the other palm, and the forearm, index finger extended, traces the path of the sun across the sky until the dominant arm rests along the top of the other forearm. If the handshape of the dominant hand is an open palm as the sign is executed, the sign is ALL DAY. The sign DAY is sometimes executed with the arms parallel, and the dominant forearm is raised up to a vertical position, index finger extended.

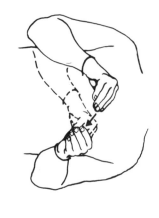

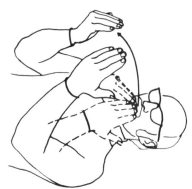

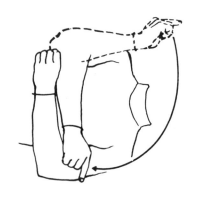

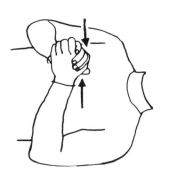

UNDER 251

The nondominant hand, palm down, and the dominant A hand, thumb up, makes small circles in a horizontal plane beneath the other palm. In an alternative execution, the dominant hand, palm down, makes small circles in a horizontal plane beneath the other hand. The nondominant hand provides a frame of reference, and the meaning is conveyed by the relation of the dominant hand to the other hand.

WORD 252

The nondominant hand is held in neutral space with the index finger extended, and the thumb and index fingers of the dominant hand measure off a portion of the index finger from the tip to about the second joint. The sign may be reduplicated as the hands move slightly to the right (or left for left-handed speakers) for the plural, WORDS.

SHOES 253

The index finger sides of both S hands are bumped against each other two or more times in neutral space. An alternative execution slips the dominant hand, palm down, into an opening formed by the nondominant C hand, palm up.

PRESIDENT, CHAIR, SUPERINTENDENT 254

The C hands, palms facing forward and outward, are brought out to the sides of the head from the region of the forehead, ending as clenched fists. This sign is used to address the CHAIR at a formal meeting. It is also used to refer to the SUPERINTENDENT of a residential school for the deaf.

FEAR, AFRAID 255

The hands are held with the palms out, fingers pointed upward, with one hand slightly forward compared to the other. They are drawn toward the body in a wavy motion that imitates the action of a person shrinking in fear from someone or something. An alternative sign FEAR, AFRAID, agitates the 5 hands, palms toward the body, as if shielding the body from harm.

GOVERNMENT 256

The index finger makes a small circle at the temple by bending the finger, and the tip of the finger is then touched to the temple. GOVERNMENT + AGENT = GOVERNOR.

TELEPHONE 257

The right Y hand is held at the cheek so that that the thumb is at the ear and the little finger at the mouth. The noun is executed as a tense, reduplicated sign at the side of the head. The verb, TELEPHONE, CALL, is a single, smooth movement that begins with the Y hand, palm down, in neutral space and brings the hand up to the side of the cheek.

FIND 258

The dominant 5 hand is lowered, palm down, in neutral space, and the thumb and index finger grasp an imaginary object, raising the hand as they do so. The sign may be executed below the nondominant palm, which conceals the imaginary object to be found, or it may pass upward through the nondominant C hand, palm to the side, providing a focus for the sign as it is executed.

WINDOW 259

The BENT B hands, palms toward the body, are held in neutral space, the dominant hand immediately above the nondominant hand, with the little finger and index finger almost touching. The hands are brought into contact with a double movement, the dominant hand coming down and the nondominant hand coming up so as to close the space between them. The action imitates the closing and opening of a window. If the hands are placed in contact and brought apart in one smooth movement, the sign is the verb, OPEN THE WINDOW. The opposite execution is CLOSE THE WINDOW.

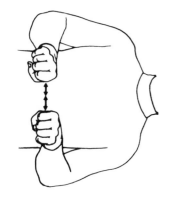 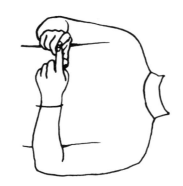 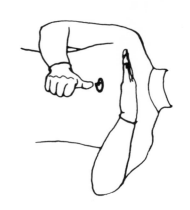

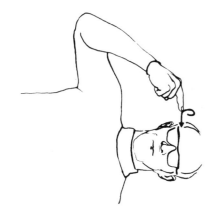 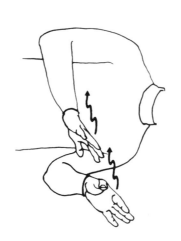 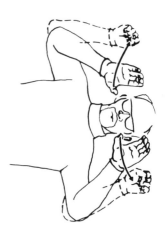

  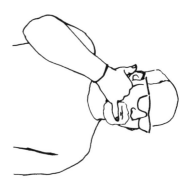

260 STUCK

The fingertips of the V hand, palm down, are jabbed into the side of the neck. The sign generally is STUCK in the sense of HELPLESS. It is also used colloquially for PREGNANT.

261 INTRODUCE

Both hands are held, palms up, some distance from each other on each side of the body. With the fingers pointing toward each other, they are brought together in front of the body as if guiding two people closer together. If one person is to be introduced specifically to another person, the movement may proceed directionally toward the person to whom the other person is being introduced.

262 LATER, AFTER WHILE

The nondominant palm is held facing sideways with the fingers pointing upward, and the thumb of the dominant L hand is placed against the palm as the index finger is moved forward in an arc with a twist of the wrist. The opposite execution, with the back of the dominant fist placed against the nondominant palm and the index finger moved backward in an arc toward the speaker's body, is PREVIOUSLY, WHILE AGO. These signs conform to the spatial rule governing tense: movements forward represent the future (LATER), and movements backward represent the past (PREVIOUSLY).

263 SIGN

The index fingers of both hands are extended in neutral space, and the hands roll over each other as they alternately circle each other. The movement is usually toward the speaker's body, but not always. This sign is often followed by the initialized sign LANGUAGE (The L hands are touched together at the thumbs and then drawn apart horizontally as they wiggle with twists of the wrists) to represent SIGN LANGUAGE. SIGN is usually a noun, referring to a specific sign/word from the ASL lexicon. The verb, SIGN, meaning *to speak in Sign Language* is executed with both S hands moving up and down alternately at the sides of the face. The execution may begin with clenched fists, opening into 5 hands with each upward movement.

264 APPLE

The thumb of the A hand or the crooked index finger of the X hand is touched to the cheek, and the hand is rocked back and forth a few times. APPLE may also be indicated by means of a natural gesture imitating taking a bite out of an imaginary apple held in the hand.

265 MILK

The fist is squeezed repeatedly in an action imitating milking a cow. Both hands may imitate the action associated with milking in alternating movements downward, or just one hand may be used with minimal downward movement.

266 SOFT

The fingers and thumb of both hands are brought slowly together several times as if squeezing something soft between the fingers.

267 PEPPER

The dominant F or O hand makes a shaking motion imitating the action of shaking PEPPER over a plate of food.

268 THING, THINGS

The dominant hand is held, palm up, in neutral space, and it is moved off to the right in a series of short, downward gestures. The singular, THING, may be indicated by a single movement of the hand toward an object or an indexed location. For the compounds, SOMETHING, EVERYTHING, and ANYTHING, the second element is often a smooth lateral movement in neutral space.

269 VOICE

The **V** hand, palm toward the throat, is brought forward in an arc from the throat. The sign may be an initialized version of SAY, SPEAK.

270 CHIEF, CHIEFLY

The dominant **A** hand, thumb up, is raised upward near the right shoulder As an adjective it refers to someone or something important. As an adverb it refers to a main or principal action. It may be added to an adjective or adverb as a comparative suffix, as in CLEAN + CHIEF = CLEANER or GOOD + CHIEF = BETTER. For the superlative, the execution raises the hand higher in space than for the comparative, as in BEST.

271 CHOOSE, PICK, SELECT

The nondominant **2** is held in neutral space, palm toward the speaker, and the dominant **F** hand imitates the action associated with evaluating and choosing one of the extended fingers of the numeral. When the choice is from a larger group, the **F** hand may make the imaginary selection from the neutral area in front of the body.

272 COLD, WINTER

The clenched fists make a shivering motion at the sides of the body. The adjective is more likely than the noun to be accompanied by facial clues appropriate for the experience of COLD.

273 ARGUE, QUARREL, FIGHT

The index fingers are pointed toward each other in neutral space, and they are moved up and down in a parallel motion by bending the wrists. If, instead of moving up and down, the index fingers are jerked apart with twists of both wrists, the sign is OPPOSED, OPPOSITE. OPPOSED + AGENT = ENEMY.

274 GIVE UP

The fists are held in neutral space with the palms down. Both hands are raised upward as they are opened into **5** hands, palms facing outward and fingers pointing up. The sign is usually accompanied by an appropriate facial expression indicating surrender.

275 READY

The **R** hands are crossed at the wrists with the palms facing downward and outward. Both hands are brought apart with a swift movement so that the final position has the **R** hands at the sides of the body. An alternative execution holds the **R** hands side by side and moves them laterally in neutral space. This latter execution is related to the sign PREPARE, which imitates the act of arranging things in order from left to right, using open hands, palms facing, in a series of downward movements. Executed in a single, swift movement from one side to the other, the sign means PREPARED, READY. For READY it may be initialized with **R** hands.

276 LEAVE, ABANDON

The two fists with palms facing in neutral space are thrown down and away from the body as they open into **5** hands, palms facing. The sign may be executed with **5** hands in the initial as well as the final position.

277 SCHOOL

The hands are clapped together in neutral space. The sign is said to be motivated by imitating a teacher clapping the hands together to call pupils to attention. The sign COLLEGE claps both hands together and then raises the dominant hand in a spiral, upward movement, palm down.

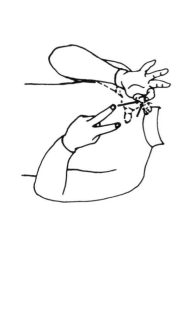
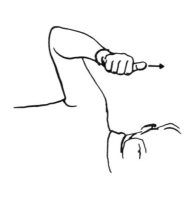
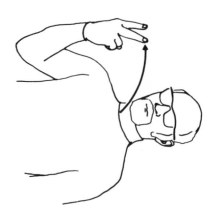

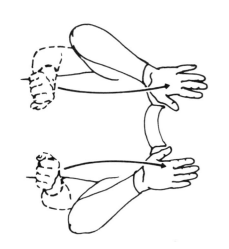

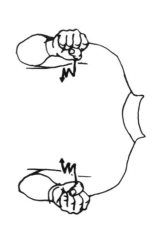

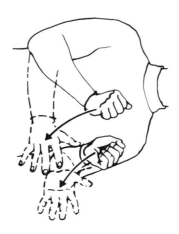
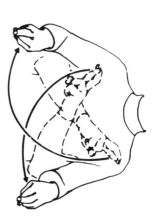

STAY, REMAIN, CONTINUE

The thumb of the dominant Y hand is placed on the thumb nail of the nondominant Y hand, and the dominant Y hand is then moved forward in neutral space, palm down, and brought to a full stop. CONTINUE may be executed with both Y hands, palms down, moving forward in neutral space. A related sign, YET, STILL, is executed with one hand: The Y hand on the chest as the hand closes to the **BABY O** position, and it is brought forward with a twist of the wrist so that the palm is down in the final position.

BOUND, ENSLAVED

The fists are crossed at the wrists as if tied up or handcuffed, and the hands make a struggling motion or a clockwise circle in neutral space. If the two hands are pulled apart forcibly, the sign is FREE, SAVE. SAVE + AGENT = SAVIOR.

UNCLE

The U hand makes two downward stroking movements at the temple. An alternative execution agitates the U hand at the temple by twisting the wrist back and forth. The location of the sign is governed by the male gender region, the forehead and temple, which is generally used for male kinship signs.

STOMACH CRAMPS, CONTRACTIONS

The **CLAW** hands are held with palms facing in neutral space in the region of the stomach or abdomen, and they are turned in opposite directions by twisting the wrists. The context will generally indicate whether the pains are specific, as in CON-TRACTIONS, or whether they are general, as in STOMACH CRAMPS.

DON'T WANT

The **CLAW** hands are held, palms up, in neutral space, and they are turned over abruptly so that the palms face away from the body. This is a negative inflection that may be applied to a few other signs in ASL. For example, the finger-tips of the palm are touched to the forehead for KNOW. If the hand is then turned abruptly away from the forehead, the sign is DON'T KNOW.

SHY

The backs of the fingers of the bent hand are rotated against the cheek as the hand is rolled forward with a twist of the wrist. Without the twist of the wrist, if the backs of the fingers trace a small circle on the cheek, the sign is PROSTI-TUTE. If the hand moves forward from the face after the backs of the fingers brush the cheek, the sign is ASHAMED. It can be used as an idiom, SHAME YOU, the equivalent of the English, *Shame on you.*

BLACK

The horizontal index finger is stroked across the eyebrow. The sign is motivated by the color of the eyebrow on the face. Other color signs that are executed by referencing an example of the color are RED (touching the lips or chin with the tip of the index finger) and WHITE (brushing the fingertips of the **5** hand on the chest as the hand closes to the **BABY O** position, motivated by feeling an imaginary white shirt.)

FAIL

The nondominant hand is held, palm up, in neutral space, and the back of the dominant V hand is stroked against the palm as the V hand moves forward from the body. This is the gen-eral sign for FAIL, the opposite of *succeed*. There is a specific sign for FAIL AN EXAM, FLUNK: the nondominant palm is held to the side, fingers pointing upward, and the thumb and index finger side of the dominant F hand is struck forcibly against it.

MOVE

The **BABY O** hands, palms down, are moved from left to right or from right to left in neutral space. There may be a hint of picking something up as the hands close to the **BABY O** position and then move in neutral space. For MOVE AWAY the hands may open into **5** hands as the hands reach a position some distance from the body.

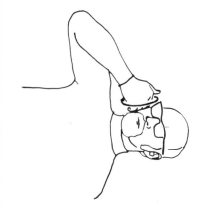 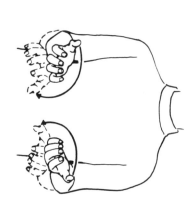 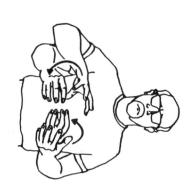

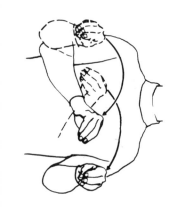 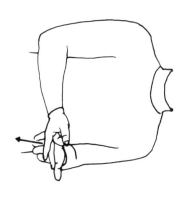 

LAW

The nondominant hand is held with the palm to the side and the fingers pointing upward, and the palm of the dominant L hand is placed twice against the nondominant palm, first near the top and then near the bottom. Related signs executed similarly are COMMANDMENT, with a C hand touched to the top and bottom of the nondominant palm. A list of COMMANDMENTS may be represented by touching the nondominant palm several times as the C hand moves from the top to the bottom of the palm. RULE, executed similarly with the R hand, and PRINCIPLE, executed similarly with the P hand. If the dominant L hand is struck forcibly against the nondominant palm, the sign is AGAINST THE LAW, ILLEGAL.

LAST, FINALLY

The nondominant little finger is extended in neutral space with the palm toward the body. The extended index finger or the extended little finger of the dominant hand is struck against it as it is brought downward in neutral space. The sign is the opposite of FIRST, executed by holding the nondominant thumb up in neutral space and striking the ball of the thumb with the extended index finger of the dominant hand.

HEART

The index fingers or the middle fingers of both hands trace a heart on the chest. Alternatively, the index or middle finger of the dominant hand may do the tracing. The region of the heart is the locus for a number of signs involving the emotions, including SORRY (a circular movement with the fist), GRIEF (the fists clenched and wrenched at the heart), HAPPY (the palm or palms are bounced off the chest near the heart), and PLEASURE (the palms are rubbed in small circles over the heart and stomach).

SOLDIER

The A hands are placed against the chest, one above the other, as if holding a rifle. SOLDIER + GROUP = ARMY.

TRULY, TRUE, REALLY, SURE

The raised index finger is placed near the mouth, and it is brought forcefully forward from the mouth. This sign is sometimes used, perhaps inappropriately, to translate literally the English copulative verb, *is, am, are, etc.* This sign has been initialized by specialists who developed **Signing Exact English** so as to yield signs for the English helping verbs. It should be recognized that ASL does not require a grammatical structure analogous to the English helping verb.

HAVE, POSSESS

The fingertips of the palms of both hands are placed against the chest. This sign does not translate the English auxiliary verb, *have, has, had.*

WALK

The hands, representing feet, make alternating steps in neutral space. Signed with index fingers and an irregular gait, the sign is CRIPPLED. Executed with fists and a slight bending of the wrist with each step, the sign may represent a heavy footed person, as in STOMP, or the gait of an animal, as in CLOMP, CLOMP. An adverb of manner may be incorporated in the execution of the verb, as in WALK SLOWLY, WALK AIMLESSLY, or WALK LABORIOUSLY. The sign may also be modified so as to represent CLIMB STAIRS or WALK UPHILL.

NAKED, BARE, EMPTY, DESERTED

The nondominant hand or fist is held, palm down, in neutral space, and the middle fingertip of the dominant hand is stroked outward along the back of the nondominant hand. The movement of the execution may be influenced by the noun that the adjective modifies; for example, an empty lot may result in the execution being extended into a circular movement of the OPEN 8 handshape, palm down, in neutral space.

SALT

The V hands are crossed over each other, palms down, in neutral space, and the fingers are wiggled, representing the appearance of salt being sprinkled from a shaker. Alternatively, one may imitate the action associated with shaking salt from an imaginary shaker.

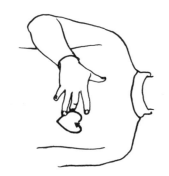 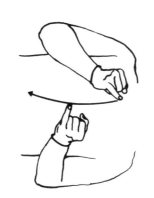 

 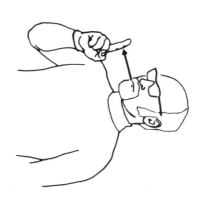 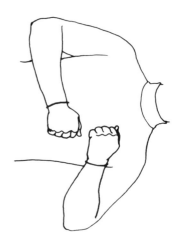

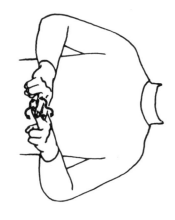 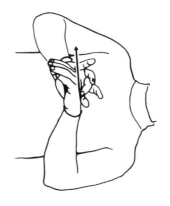 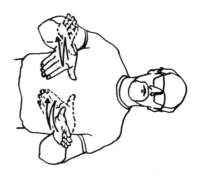

TERRIBLE, AWFUL

The O or F hands are placed at the sides of the head, and they are opened quickly into 5 hands as the hands are raised above eye level. The initial position may begin with 8 hands. The sign may be executed directionally. For example, to indicate that a plate of food is AWFUL, the movement of the sign may be from neutral space toward the imaginary plate of food.

LONG TIME

The fingertip of the L hand is drawn slowly up the nondominant arm from the wrist toward the elbow. The sign TIME may be added after the execution, but it is not necessary. The sign may stand alone as LONG TIME.

NOT YET

The dominant hand is held near the waist with the fingers pointing downward, and the hand is moved back two or more times by bending the wrist. The sign acts as a temporal adverb, modifying the verb. For example, I NOT-YET SEE THAT BEFORE could be translated, *I have not seen that before.*

AUTUMN, FALL

The nondominant forearm is held in a vertical or diagonal position in neutral space, and the dominant hand, palm down, is stroked downward along the outside of the other forearm near the elbow. The sign is said to be motivated by leaves falling from a tree, whose trunk is represented by the nondominant forearm.

COMPLAIN

The fingertips of the CLAW hand, palm toward the body, are struck against the chest. Both hands may be used in an alternating execution. If the fingertips of the CLAW hands are in contact with the chest as the body squirms restlessly, the sign is UNCOMFORTABLE. If the CLAW hand makes a small clockwise circle on the chest, accompanied by an appropriate facial expression, the sign is DISGUSTED.

MOST

The nondominant A hand is held, thumb up, in neutral space, and the dominant A hand, thumb, up, brushes past it as it moves upward in neutral space. This sign is related to CHIEF, CHIEFLY, which raises the dominant A hand, thumb up, up above eye level near the head.

RIGHT, MORALLY RIGHT, ALL RIGHT

The nondominant hand is held, palm up, in neutral space, and the dominant hand, palm to the side and fingers pointing forward, is moved in a straight line down the middle of the nondominant hand. Executed with the H hand, the sign is HONEST. If the execution ends with an erratic movement off to the side, the sign is PERVERSE, WRONG. This sign does not translate *right* in the sense of *correct*, which is signed by striking the dominant fist, index finger extended, on the top of the nondominant fist, index finger extended. Executed with a serious facial expression, the sign is MORALLY RIGHT, UPRIGHT. Executed casually the sign is ALL RIGHT, OK.

JESUS

The middle finger of the dominant hand is touched to the middle of the other palm, and the middle finger of the nondominant hand is touched to the middle of the dominant palm. The sign calls attention to the *stigmata*, or nail prints, in the hands of Jesus. JESUS + BOOK = BIBLE. JESUS + AGENT = CHRISTIAN.

KEEP

The dominant K hand is touched to the top of the nondominant K hand once or twice. Executed with both hands in contact and moved in a circle out from the body in a vertical plane, the sign is BE CAREFUL. Executed with the hands in contact as they make a counterclockwise circle in a horizontal plane, the sign is SUPERVISE. SUPERVISE + AGENT = SUPERVISOR. The signs SUPERVISE and SUPERVISOR have special significance to many deaf people, since they are used to refer to the dormitory counselors, who were very important people in their lives if they attended residential schools.

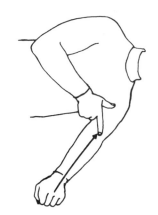

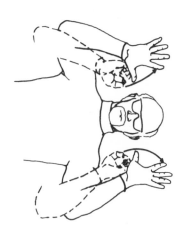

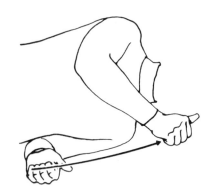

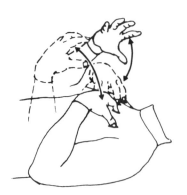

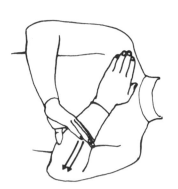

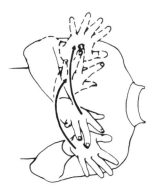

NUMBER, NUMERAL

Both hands form the BABY O handshape. The fingertips of the dominant hand, palm down, are touched against the fingertips of the nondominant hand, and, then, the hands change places with a twist of both wrists, and the fingertips of the nondominant hand, palm down, are touched against the fingertips of the dominant hand.

JUDGE, COURT

The two F hands, palms facing, are moved alternately up and down in neutral space. A related sign, WORTH, VALUE, raises the two F hands up so as to meet at the midline in neutral space. If the F hands, facing outward, are flung apart, ending as 5 hands, the sign is WORTHLESS.

MY, MINE

The open palm is placed against the speaker's chest. The open palm is the handshape associated with the possessive pronoun in ASL. It is executed directionally for YOUR (sing.), HIS, HER, HERS, ITS, YOUR (plural) and THEIR. OUR, OURS is executed by touching the thumb edge of the right hand to the right shoulder and then moving the hand around so that the little finger edge of the hand touches the left shoulder. (Left handed speakers would use the left hand, touching the left and then the right shoulder.)

PROCRASTINATE, KEEP PUTTING OFF

The F hands are held side by side in neutral space with the palms facing, and the dominant F hand is moved forward from the nondominant hand in a series of small arcs which extend far from the body. If the sign is executed with a single arc forward from the body, the sign is POSTPONE.

SIN

Both fists are held in neutral space with the index fingers extended. The index fingers simultaneously trace small circles in a vertical plane in front of the body.

HAPPY

The palm is brushed upward against the chest over the heart two or more times. Both hands may be used, the one positioned slightly above the chest and both striking the chest simultaneously. If the palm is rubbed in a clockwise circle over the heart, the sign is PLEASE. If both hands make circles on the chest and stomach, the sign is ENJOY, PLEASURE.

BORROW

The dominant K hand is placed on top of the nondominant K hand in neutral space some distance from the body, and both hands are moved in an arc toward the speaker's body by bending the wrists. Executed in the opposite direction, away from the speaker's body, the sign is LEND. In an alternative execution, the wrists are not bent, but both hands are simply moved toward the body (BORROW) or away from the body (LEND) in a small arc. LEND may be executed directionally, toward the person to whom the loan is being considered.

GO

The index fingers pointed in the general direction of the sign, are brought down and out in an arc, ending with the fingers pointing forward. In another version of the sign, the index fingers pointing toward the body. The index fingers are rolled over each other as they proceed outward from the body. This sign may be executed directionally, consistent with the spatial organization of the discourse. There is also a fingerspelled sign, G-O, executed with a movement away from the body. If the index fingers are rolled over one another as they are brought toward the body, the sign is COME. To reverse the first execution so as to yield COME, the index fingers are brought up and toward the body in an arc, ending so that they point toward the speaker's body.

CLOTHES

The fingertips of the 5 hands are brushed downward on the upper part of the chest two or more times. Brushed upward on the upper legs the sign is TROUSERS, SLACKS. Brushed upward on each forearm, first with one hand and then with the other, the sign is STOCKINGS.

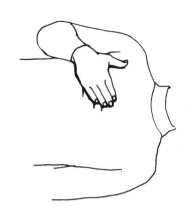
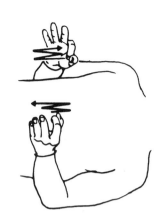
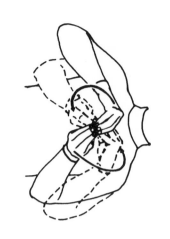

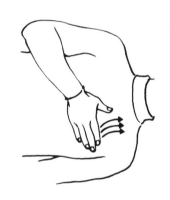
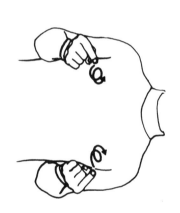

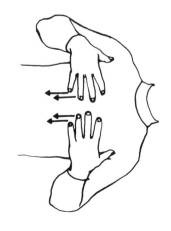

FRIEND

The index fingers are locked together, first with the dominant hand above the nondominant hand and then the reverse. If the index fingers are locked together and squeezed tightly or tugged, the sign is CLOSE FRIEND, GOOD FRIEND.

WEAK

The nondominant hand is held, palm up, in neutral space. The fingertips of the dominant hand are placed in the other palm, and they are bent as the dominant hand is pushed toward the left. The action suggests that the fingers are unable to withstand the pressure because they are WEAK. If the sign is executed on the forehead, the sign is FEEBLE-MINDED.

MEASURE

The thumb tips of the Y hands, palms down, are touched together, as the extended little fingers measure off an expanse of space. The sign may be executed in the direction of the object to be measured. If the hands are twisted back and forth in opposite directions by twisting both wrists, the sign is DRAFTSMAN, ENGINEER.

FIRE

The 5 hands are held with the fingers pointing upward and the palms toward the speaker. The fingers are wiggled as the hands move upward in neutral space. If the hands are raised alternately as the fingers wiggle, the sign is the verb, BURN. The right hand may be used alone to represent a flame as the left hand provides a frame of reference. For example, executed over the raised index finger, it is CANDLE, and under the flat palm it is STOVE.

BECAUSE

The index fingertip of the L hand or the fingertips of the open hand are touched to the forehead, and then the hand is raised up from the forehead, ending in the thumbs-up A handshape. This sign is used less frequently in ASL than in English, since causes or reasons or often given after asking the rhetorical question, WHY? eliminating any need for a causal clause. The sign may be a compound: THINK + CHIEF or KNOW + CHIEF, meaning *I know something of importance.*

DOLLAR

The nondominant hand is held in neutral space with the palm to the side and fingers pointing forward. The dominant hand grasps the middle of the nondominant hand and slides forward and off the end of the hand. The sign is said to be motivated by smoothing out a dollar bill. There is an idiomatic execution in ASL for indicating small amounts of money without using the sign DOLLAR: the numeral is presented palm out, and it is then swept in a downward arc and raised up again with the numeral toward the face. This execution may be used for $1, $2, $3, ... $10. For larger dollar amounts, the sign DOLLAR is executed either before or after the numeral (DOLLAR 25 or 25 DOLLAR = $25).

PEOPLE

The P hands are moved alternately up and down or in a slightly circular motion in neutral space. The circular movement comes toward the speaker's body. The sign is always plural. For PERSON the two P hands are drawn downward vertically in a parallel motion in neutral space.

WHISKEY

The index and little finger are extended as the thumb holds the middle and fourth fingers tucked in the palm. The little finger side of this handshape is then tapped against the back of the nondominant fist. The sign is said to be motivated by the small size of a shot glass of WHISKEY.

SUNDAY

The hands are held up with the palms facing outward and fingers pointing upward in neutral space. The hands make small circles in a vertical plane in opposite directions. A regional sign in Ohio presents the hands with the palms toward the face and the index fingers touching. Both hands are turned outward one or more times. MONDAY through SATURDAY are initialized signs; the appropriate letter of the manual alphabet is circled as the hand is held near the shoulder. The palm may face outward or backward, depending on the context. To distinguish THURSDAY from TUESDAY, THURSDAY circles the letter H in neutral space. An idiomatic execution for THURSDAY rubs the inside of the middle finger of the H hand against the thumb as the finger moves back and forth in contact with the thumb.

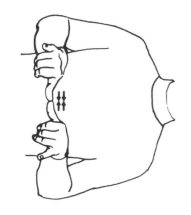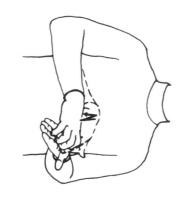

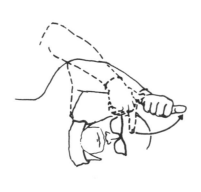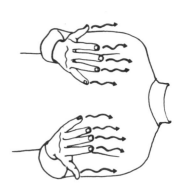

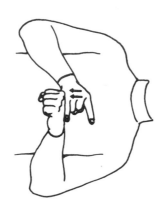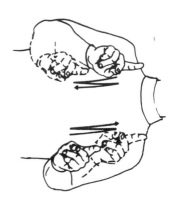

323 FISH

The nondominant hand, palm to the side and fingers pointing forward, is placed in contact with the inside of the wrist of the dominant hand, which also has the fingers pointing forward and the palm to the side. The dominant hand, representing the fish, is flopped back and forth or moves slightly forward or backward as it wiggles with a twisting of the wrist. Alternatively, the dominant hand may serve as a classifier for a fish, and it can represent a fish by imitating its movement through the water.

324 POOR

The nondominant forearm is raised up in neutral space, and the dominant hand grasps the elbow and slides off, ending with the fingers clustered together. The sign is said to be motivated by the holes in the elbows of a sweater worn by a person too poor to have it mended or replaced.

325 MIXED, CONFUSED

The CLAW hands are held in neutral space with the palms facing, and they are circled in a horizontal plane, the one following the other in a counterclockwise direction. If the CLAW hands, palms facing, are turned over abruptly with a twist of both wrists, the sign is WRECK, ACCIDENT.

326 WEEK

The nondominant hand is held palm up in neutral space, and the dominant L hand or the dominant fist with the index finger extended is moved outward along the nondominant palm. This sign can be inflected for number by presenting the appropriate numeral on the dominant hand, as in TWO WEEKS, THREE WEEKS, etc. It can also be inflected for tense by extending the movement forward from the palm for the future and backward over the shoulder for the past. From this inflection one can construct TWO WEEKS AGO, THREE WEEKS FROM NOW, LAST WEEK, NEXT WEEK, etc. Reduplicated, the sign is WEEKLY, EVERY WEEK.

327 SHEEP

The nondominant arm is held horizontally in neutral space, representing the back of the sheep. The dominant V hand, representing scissors or shears, is moved up the nondominant forearm as it makes cutting motions, as if shearing a sheep.

328 MONDAY

The M hand, palm facing the speaker, makes a small circle in a vertical plane near the shoulder. If the context requires an emphatic execution, the palm faces the listener. A similar execution is used with the T hand for TUESDAY, with the W hand for WEDNESDAY, with the H hand for THURSDAY, with the F hand for FRIDAY, and with the S hand for SATURDAY. MONDAY can be inflected with a downward movement for MONDAYS, EVERY MONDAY, ON MONDAYS. The same inflection can also be applied to the other days of the week.

329 POTATO

The nondominant fist is held palm down in neutral space, and the fingertips of the inverted V of the dominant hand, representing a fork, are touched to the back of the other fist. The sign is said to be motivated by testing potatos to see if they are done.

330 EXCEPT, SPECIAL, EXCEPTIONAL

The raised index finger of the nondominant hand or the index fingertip of the nondominant 5 hand is grasped by the thumb and index finger of the dominant hand and pulled upward. The sign represents singling out someone special or exceptional.

331 BETWEEN

The nondominant hand is held with the palm to the side and the fingers pointing forward, thumb up. The little finger edge of the dominant hand is placed BETWEEN the thumb and the first knuckle of the index finger of the nondominant hand. BOTHER is executed similarly, except that the dominant hand strikes the other hand forcefully two or more times.

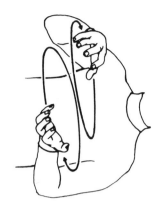 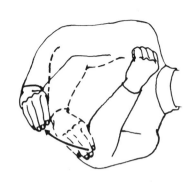 

 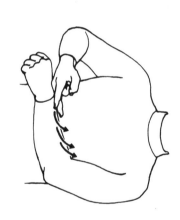 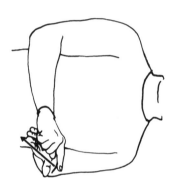

  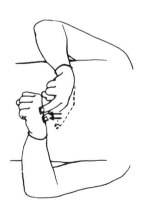

332 SING, SONG, MUSIC

The nondominant hand is held with the palm toward the face, as if it is holding music, and the right hand is moved rhythmically back and forth as if keeping time or directing a band or chorus. Executed with a **P** hand, the sign is POETRY.

333 WHICH? OR

The two **A** hands, thumbs up, are moved up and down alternately in neutral space. Executed with a questioning facial expression, the sign is the interrogative, WHICH? WHICH ONE? The eye gaze may be directed at the hands as the sign is executed. The sign is related to MAYBE, executed with open hands, palms up, JUDGE, executed with **F** hands, palms facing, and DOUBT, executed with clenched fists, palms down.

334 HONOR

The dominant **H** hand is drawn downward and outward in an arc, beginning in the region of the forehead. Executed with the **R** hand, the sign is RESPECT.

335 MEMORIZE

The fingertips of the dominant **5** hand, palm toward the face, graze the forehead as the hand is brought forward from the head and clenched into a fist. The sign represents taking something from the head and holding on to it.

336 SENIOR

The nondominant **5** hand is held with the palm toward the speaker and the fingers pointing to the side. The dominant **5** hand, palm down, is touched to the tip of the extended thumb of the nondominant hand. This sign refers to the senior year of college at Gallaudet University. Signs for the PREPARATORY YEAR, FRESHMAN, SOPHOMORE, and JUNIOR years, respectively, touch the tip of the dominant index finger to the extended little finger, fourth finger, middle finger, and index finger of the nondominant **5** hand presented with the palm to the speaker and fingers pointing to the side.

337 DOUBT

The fists are clenched, palms down, in neutral space, and they are moved up and down alternately. An alternative sign for DOUBT implying SKEPTICISM or SUSPICION points the fingers of the **V** hand toward the eyes and then bends the fingers several times so that the fingertips move up and down in front of the eyes. This sign may be executed with a single movement, beginning with the fingers pointing toward the eyes and ending in the BENT **V** handshape as the hand is drawn forward and downward from the face.

338 SUMMARIZE, CONDENSE, ABBREVIATE

The **C** or **CLAW** hands are held at the sides of the body with the palms facing, and they are brought together at the midline, ending with one hand above the other as the fists are clenched.

339 COOK

The back and the palm of the dominant hand are slapped alternately into the upturned nondominant palm. The sign may also be used for KITCHEN. COOK + AGENT = CHEF, COOK. BAKE is executed by holding the nondominant hand, palm down and fingers pointing to the side in neutral space to represent an oven, and the dominant hand, palm up and fingers pointing forward, moves under the nondominant palm, as if placing something in the oven.

340 FAR, FAR AWAY

The nondominant **A** hand, thumb up, is held in neutral space as a frame of reference, and the dominant **A** hand, thumb up, is placed near the nondominant hand and then moved in an arc away from the body. An emphatic execution first raises the dominant **A** hand in neutral space and then moves it far from the body, turning the head aside as the sign is executed.

 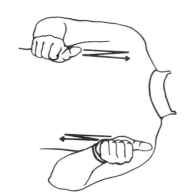 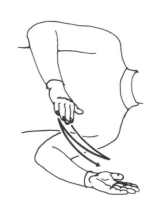

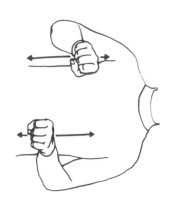 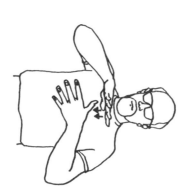 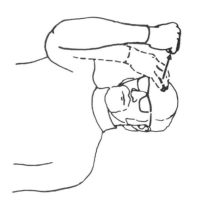

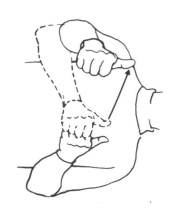 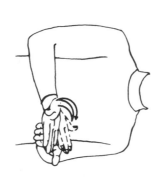 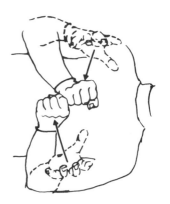

SPOON 347

The nondominant hand is held palm up in neutral space. The tips of the extended index and middle fingers are brought near the lips, and then the backs of these extended fingers are placed on the upturned nondominant palm. The first element of the compound may be deleted.

GRANDMOTHER 341

The thumb of the 5 hand is touched to the chin, and the hand is then moved forward from the chin in two small arcs. The hand may turn so that the palm is up as the sign is executed. An alternative execution uses both hands for the second element of the sign: after the sign MOTHER is executed, the hands are placed palms up in neutral space and then moved back over the shoulder. This second element of the compound may be motivated by holding a baby and referencing the past. GRANDFATHER is executed similarly, but the sign begins with the thumb touched to the forehead or near the forehead.

PAIN 344

The index fingers of both hands are extended with the palms toward the body, and the index fingers are jabbed toward each other as the wrists are slightly twisted. The sign may be executed near the forehead for HEADACHE or at the stomach for STOMACH ACHE.

GOOD 342

The fingertips of the dominant hand are brought near the mouth, and the back of the dominant hand is then dropped into the nondominant palm. The sign may be executed with only the dominant hand. If the hand is turned away from the face after it references the mouth, the sign is BAD. GOOD + CHIEF = BETTER.

OTHER, ANOTHER 348

The dominant A hand, thumb up, is moved off to the side in an arc. The wrist is twisted as the sign is executed so that the thumb points off to the side in the final position.

BEER 345

The thumb of the dominant Y hand, palm to the side, is tipped up to the mouth as if lifting a stein of beer. The sign may be executed by moving the thumb of the A hand toward the mouth. If the A hand is jabbed repeatedly toward the mouth, the sign is DRUNK or TAVERN. DRUNK may also be executed by weaving the right Y hand forward from the face as if to imitate a staggering gait.

IMPORTANT, WORTH, VALUE 343

The F hands are held some distance apart in neutral space with the palms facing, and they are brought upward and toward the midline as the wrists turn so that the palms are down as the hands come into contact. An alternative execution maintains the palms facing each other throughout the execution, and contact is made by the tips of the thumbs and index fingers. An alternative sign IMPORTANT places the dominant hand with the I handshape on the back of the nondominant fist, and both hands are raised upward in neutral space.

YEAR 349

The fists are held in neutral space, one above the other, and the dominant fist circles the other, ending on top and in contact with the other fist. This sign can be inflected for number by presenting the appropriate numeral on the dominant hand as the sign is executed: ONE YEAR, TWO YEARS, THREE YEARS, etc. The sign may also be inflected for tense, deleting the circle around the other fist and moving the appropriate numeral forward from the nondominant fist or back over the shoulder. This results in NEXT YEAR, TWO YEARS FROM NOW, LAST YEAR, TWO YEARS AGO, etc. There is an idiomatic execution for LAST YEAR that holds the dominant hand palm up with the thumb and index finger extended, and the index finger is wagged back toward the right shoulder.

SINCE, UNTIL NOW, FOR SOME TIME 346

The index fingers of both hands are brought up over the right shoulder, and the hands are then brought forward and down in neutral space, ending with the index fingers extended forward and the palms down as in the final position for HAPPEN. The sign implies an action that began in the past and continued for a duration, perhaps up to the present. I WORK PRINTER SINCE 24 YEARS would be translated *I have worked as a printer for 24 years*. I NO WORK SINCE PAST MONDAY would be translated *I have not worked since last Monday*.

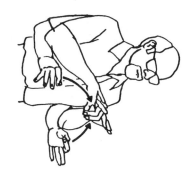 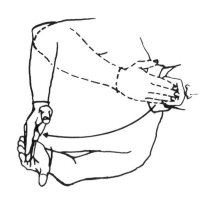 

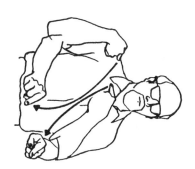  

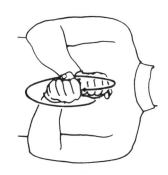  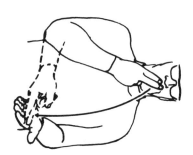

350 BROKE, OUT OF MONEY

The little finger edge of the right BENT B hand, palm down, is struck against the right side of the neck. Left handed speakers would revise the execution accordingly. This is a colloquial expression and applies only to one's financial condition.

351 THIS, THAT

The nondominant hand is held in neutral space with the palm up, and the dominant Y hand, palm down, is struck against the other palm. This is the demonstrative pronoun in ASL. It may be executed without support from the nondominant hand, and it may be executed directionally, toward its antecedent. Plural executions may sweep the Y hand in an arc or make discrete references to different indexed locations. THIS and THESE reference locations close to the body; THAT and THOSE reference locations farther from the body.

352 AGAIN

The nondominant hand is held with the palm toward the speaker's face, and the dominant hand, palm up, is brought up and toward the nondominant palm, ending with the fingertips of the dominant hand making contact with the palm. A reduplicated execution, touching the fingertips of the dominant hand to the nondominant palm repeatedly as they move up the palm, is the sign OFTEN. The motivation for OFTEN may be the notion of something happening AGAIN, AGAIN, and AGAIN.

353 BLUE

The dominant B hand, fingers pointing up, is agitated in neutral space by twisting the wrist. For DEEP BLUE a lateral movement may be added to the sign as it is executed. Similar initialized signs result in the color signs YELLOW, GREEN, and PURPLE.

354 JEALOUS, ENVY

The little finger or the index finger of the dominant hand is clenched lightly between the teeth, or the little finger or index finger of the dominant hand makes a small *J* at the side of the mouth. The English word *covet* in the Ten Commandments is sometimes signed with a compound, JEALOUS + WANT.

355 OVERCOME, DEFEAT

The dominant fist is moved downward forcefully over the horizontal nondominant forearm. The right wrist is bent at the final position, implying forceful subjugation. A related sign thrusts the dominant C hand over the nondominant forearm for FORCE.

356 WARM

The dominant closed hand is held near the mouth with the fingers toward the mouth. The hand is gently opened into a 5 hand as the hand moves up and away from the mouth. The sign may be motivated by the warmth of the human breath. HOT is signed in the same location: the CLAW hand is held with the palm toward the mouth, and it is turned quickly outward. There may be a forceful expulsion of breath as the sign is executed.

357 WORRY

The hands are held in neutral space with the palms facing, and they are moved alternately past the face in a circular pattern. The sign may be executed as an initialized sign with W handshapes.

358 EARTH

The nondominant fist is held palm down in neutral space, and the thumb and middle fingers grasp the outside knuckles of the fist. Both wrists may be bent slightly so as to produce a rocking motion, representing the movement of the earth on its axis. If the hands are held in their initial position and shaken back and forth, the sign is EARTHQUAKE.

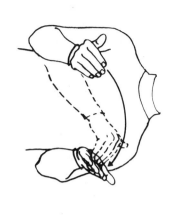 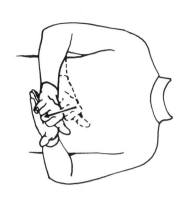 

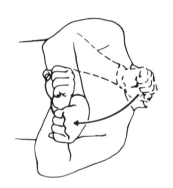 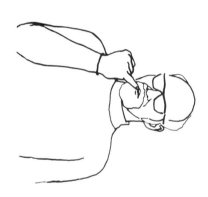 

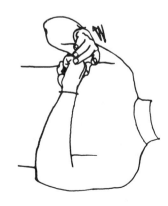 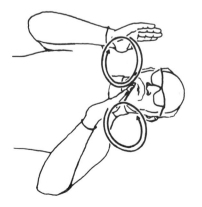 

WRITE 359

The nondominant hand is held, palm up, in neutral space, and the dominant hand imitates the act of writing on it, holding an imaginary pencil between the thumb and index finger. The sign is used similarly for the signs READ (with the nondominant palm is used similarly for the signs READ (with the dominant **V** hand), DRAW (with the little finger of the dominant hand), NOTICE (with the index fingertip of the dominant hand), PRINT (with the thumb and index finger of the dominant hand tapped together), and several other related signs.

FUTURE, WILL, LATER 360

The dominant hand, palm to the side and thumb up, is moved forward from the shoulder in neutral space. The REMOTE FUTURE is indicated by moving the hand farther from the body. The NEAR FUTURE, SOON, is indicated by shortening the movement, locating the hand closer to the cheek, hunching the shoulder or shoulders, and squinting the side of the face. This sign can be used in different positions of a sentence relative to the verb, unlike the English, *shall*, *will*, which ordinarily occur immediately before the verb they modify.

SHORT TIME 361

The fingers of both **H** hands are extended with the palms toward the speaker and the extended fingers crossed at the knuckles. The extended fingers of the dominant hand are moved back and forth between the knuckles of the extended fingers of the nondominant hand. If the fingers of the dominant hand move forward and off the front of the other fingers in one, brief gesture, the sign is BRIEF, QUICK.

FALSE 362

The upright index finger, palm to the side, is moved across the mouth from right to left (left to right for left handed speakers). The sign is related to two other signs, LIE, DECEIVE, which moves the horizontal index finger from right to left across the mouth, and FALSE, FAKE, LIE, which moves the fingers of the **BENT B** hand from right to left across the mouth. Both **BENT B** hands can be used, moving alternately in opposite directions across the mouth.

COMPARE 363

The dominant hand, fingers pointing up, is brought before the face with a twist of the wrist so that the eyes can see the palm, and then the nondominant hand does the same. The right and left hands alternate, each offering an opportunity for inspection and comparison.

GROW, SPRING 364

The nondominant hand is held in an **O** handshape with the opening at the top, and the fingers of the dominant **BABY O** are thrust up through the opening of the nondominant hand, opening into the **5** handshape as they do so. The sign is also used for the SPRING of the year. If the execution is reduplicated in short movements, the sign is GRASS.

FREEZE 365

The **5** hands, palms down, are curled into **CLAW** hands, representing the solidifying effect of freezing.

LOVE 366

The arms with clenched fists are crossed at the wrists over the heart. An alternative execution uses crossed palms over the heart. When the fists are squeezed for emphasis, the sign is VERY FOND.

HARD 367

The nondominant fist is held in neutral space, palm down, and the middle finger knuckle of the dominant **BENT V** hand is struck against the back of the other fist. The same handshape with the knuckle of the index finger struck against the bridge of the nose is STRICT.

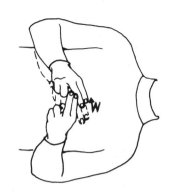

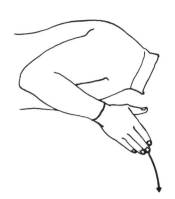

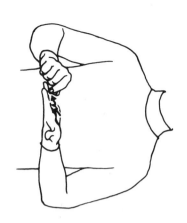

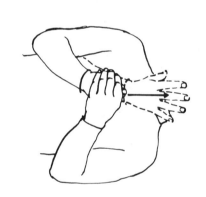

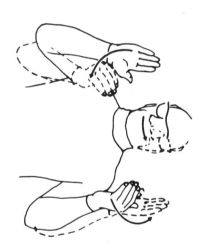

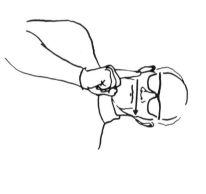

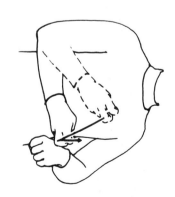

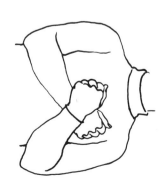

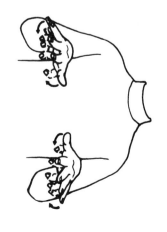

POLICEMAN, COP   368

The C hand is placed on the left side of the chest where a policeman's badge is worn. An alternative execution places the fingertips of the cupped CLAW hand on the left side of the chest. One of the signs for FIREMAN is motivated similarly: the C hand is placed on the forehead, where the fireman's badge is located on his or her cap.

374

HUMBLE   368

The nondominant hand is held just below eye level with the palm down or with the palm toward the speaker's body. The index finger edge of the dominant hand, palm to the side and fingers pointing up, is placed against or near the mouth, and then the dominant hand slides down and along or under the other palm. The head and shoulders may be bowed slightly as the sign is executed.

CAT   371

The thumbs and index fingers of both hands are brought together at the sides of the mouth and trace whiskers out from the cheeks. The sign may be executed with one hand. Another member of the cat family, TIGER, is executed similarly: the fingertips of the 5 hands trace stripes from the middle to the outside of the face.

WHO?   369

The index finger traces a small circle around the rounded lips. In an alternative sign, the thumb of the L hand is touched to the chin, and the index finger is wiggled as the lips are shaped so as to ask WHO? Still another sign closes the 5 hand into the BABY O handshape at the lips as they are rounded to say WHO? This sign is generally used as an interrogative pronoun.

CAN'T   372

The dominant index finger, palm down, is swing downward so as to strike the tip of the nondominant index finger extended palm down in neutral space. In an alternative execution, the nondominant hand is held palm up, and its extended index finger swings up to meet the other index finger coming down, with the result that they make contact as the tips of the fingers pass each other in opposite directions. A reduplicated execution with the nondominant hand stationary and palm down is sometimes used for DON'T DO THAT, AGAINST THE RULES. In some contexts the sign is IMPOSSIBLE.

ALWAYS   370

The dominant forearm is held at the side of the body or near the shoulder with the index finger extended. The index finger traces a clockwise circle two or more times (counterclockwise for a left handed speaker). A compound formed by ALWAYS + a one-handed execution of STAY is sometimes used for ETERNITY, FOREVER.

CAR   375

The hands imitate turning a steering wheel. The VEHICLE classifier handshape may also be used to represent a CAR; namely, the hand is held with the palm to the side, the middle and index fingers extended, and the thumb raised. The VEHI-CLE handshape is used for GARAGE (moved under the non-dominant palm), PARK (placed on the nondominant palm) and PARKING LOT (placed repeatedly side by side on the non-dominant palm), and several verbs of motion involving a car: BACK UP, PULL OVER, TURN A CORNER, WEAVE DOWN THE ROAD, RUN INTO THE DITCH, etc. CAR is often executed as a fingerspelled sign, C-A-R. The verb, DRIVE, grasps the imaginary steering wheel in both hands and moves the hands forward from the body into neutral space.

FUNNY   376

The fingertips of the dominant H hand brush downward on the tip of the nose several times. The thumb may be extended as the sign is executed. A related sign, FUN, touches the finger-tips of the dominant H hand to the nose and then slaps the extended index and middle fingers of both hands on top of each other alternately several times.

EXPERIENCE   373

The dominant 5 hand is held at the side of the head with the fingertips near or touching the temple. The hand closes to the BABY O handshape as the hand is drawn sideways away from the side of the head. The movement may be made twice.

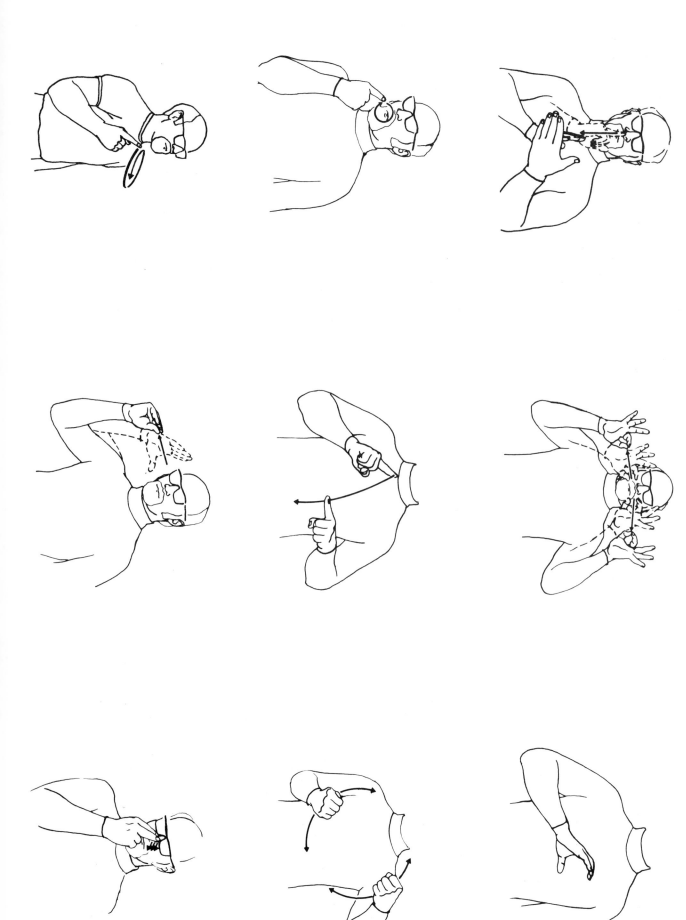

377

PROVE, PROOF, EVIDENCE

The back of the dominant hand is dropped forcefully into the upturned nondominant palm held in neutral space. For an emphatic execution, the dominant hand may be brought up from a palm-down position in neutral space, turned over, and then dropped into the nondominant palm.

378

ANSWER

The extended index fingers of both hands are held upright with the palms facing, except that the nondominant hand is farther forward in neutral space than the dominant hand. The dominant hand is located near the mouth in the initial position. Both index fingers are brought forward from the mouth in an arc made by bending both wrists simultaneously. The location of the sign is influenced by the mouth as the source of speech.

379

BEAR

The arms are crossed with the palms at the shoulders, and the CLAW hands scratch repeatedly the front of the shoulders. This sign is used solely for the animal, BEAR, and not for the verb, *bear, carry.*

380

NO

The index and middle finger of the dominant hand are brought into contact with the thumb. The sign may be an elision of the fingerspelled N-O. Two hands may be used for emphasis. This sign is restricted to the meaning *to say no.* It is not used for the adjective NO, NONE, which is executed by drawing the 0 hands apart horizontally in neutral space.

381

SEE

The V hand is held with the fingertips pointing to the eyes, and the hand is brought forward from the face. The sign may be executed directionally, with the movement proceeding toward the seen object. The opposite execution, the fingertips of the V hand jabbed at the eyes, is BLIND. If the fingers of the V hand are turned out, away from the face, the sign is LOOK, LOOK AT. This sign is generally directed toward the object of the verb, including the speaker, as in LOOK AT ME. Various adverbs of manner may be incorporated in the execution so as to yield STARE, LOOK AROUND, LOOK BACK, LOOK FORWARD, *etc.*

382

HEALTHY, BRAVE, STRONG

The fingertips of both 5 hands are touched to the chest, and both hands are then brought forward from the chest forcefully as they close into clenched fists. The context is the main distinction between the various nuances of meaning that the sign can take on. An alternative sign STRONG holds both hands, fingers curled and palms facing, at one side of the body in neutral space and moves them to the midpoint in a tense arc as they are clenched tightly into fists.

383

SAY

The horizontal extended index finger is moved forward and outward from the mouth in a single, smooth movement or in two or more brief movements. The single execution is used for TELL, and it may be executed directionally. A forceful execution of TELL is used for COMMAND. The reduplicated execution is also used for the noun, HEARING PERSON. It is noteworthy that the deaf community references hearing people not by a sign that points to their ears, calling attention to the fact that they can hear, but, instead, references the fact that hearing people are able to speak. It is speech more than hearing that separates the deaf and hearing communities. Deaf people sign; hearing people talk.

384

ANGRY

The CLAW hands, palms toward the body, are torn upward toward the shoulders in a forceful manner. The degree of anger to be represented can be indicated by the force or vigor of the execution and by the accompanying facial expression and body language. An alternative sign for ANGRY, CROSS holds the CLAW hand with the palm toward the face and bends the fingers either once forcefully or several times. The facial expression displays a PEEVED or CROSS expression.

385

NAME

The extended fingers of the two H hands, palms toward the body, are crossed at the knuckles to form an X. To represent the verb, CALL, NAME, the hands may move forward from the body before making contact. The noun may involve a double contact with brief separations of the fingers.

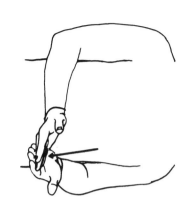

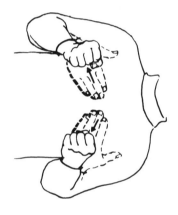
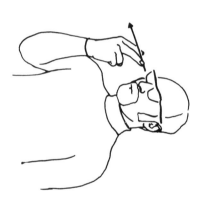

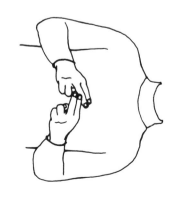

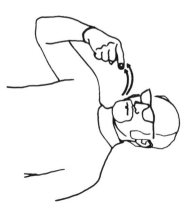

FORGIVE, EXCUSE, EXCUSE ME

The nondominant hand is held, palm up, in neutral space, and the fingertips of the dominant hand, palm down, are brushed against the edge of the other palm two or more times. This sign is used in the same way as the common English expression, *Excuse me.*

GOLD

The index finger points to the ear lobe, and the **Y** hand is then wiggled off to the side of the head. The two elements of the sign refer, first, to a part of the body where gold is likely to be worn (earrings) and, then, to the shiny appearance of polished gold. By association wit the Gold Rush, the same sign is also used for CALIFORNIA, although the execution may use the same **OPEN 8** handshape for the entire sign. An agreed-upon sign for SILVER is harder to document. One version is a compound formed by WHITE + clasped hands shaking imaginary coins in neutral space. Another touches the back of the nondominant fist with the tip of the middle finger of the **OPEN 8** handshape and then wiggles the handshape as it moves up from the fist. In other contexts, this is the sign SHINY.

INTERESTED, INTERESTING

The two **5** hands, palms toward the body, the dominant hand above the nondominant hand, move forward and outward from the body as the thumb and index fingers are brought into contact, ending as **F** hands, palms toward the body. The handshape used may change from the **OPEN 8** to the **CLOSED 8** position. Executed with one hand, the signs are LIKE, BE ATTRACTED TO. An alternative execution for INTERESTED begins with the dominant **5** hand near the face and the nondominant **5** hand near the chest, and the hands close into **A** hands as they move forward from the face and chest.

DUMB, STUPID

The knuckles of the fist are knocked against the forehead one or more times. The sign is generally derogatory. An alternative sign, IGNORANT, places the back of the **V** hand against the forehead.

NEVER

The right hand, palm out, is waved to the right, then down and to the left, and then to the right again in neutral space. The sign is related to DON'T, which crosses the arms, palms facing outward, and brings them apart forcefully in neutral space. NEVER may be a reduplicated one-handed version of DON'T, implying NO, NO, NO.

TEASE, HARM, SPOIL

The **X** hands are held with the palms to the sides, knuckles pointing forward, and the dominant hand above and behind the nondominant hand. The dominant **X** hand is moved forward forcefully, scraping the top of the nondominant **X** hand. The movement may be repeated two or more times. **A** hands may be used. The various nuances of the sign, from TEASE to RUIN, are conveyed by nonmanual signals, including facial expression, body language, and the force or vigor of the execution.

NOTHING

The **0** hands, palms facing outward in neutral space, are drawn apart horizontally, ending as **5** hands. An alternative execution holds the fist, palm down, under or near the chin, and the hand opens to the **5** handshape, palm down, as the hand is thrown forward and downward from the chin. A third execution holds both **F** hands in neutral space with the palms facing outward, and they are shaken back and forth by bending both wrists. The facial expression may include pushed out lips and squinted eyes.

USE UP, USED UP, ALL GONE

The nondominant arm is held horizontally with the palm down or with the palm to the side, fingers pointing forward. The dominant **C** hand, palm to the side, is placed with the little finger edge in contact with the nondominant arm or hand. The dominant hand is scraped along the top of the other hand as it moves forward and outward into neutral space, ending as a clenched fist. The same sign may be executed along the extended nondominant index finger. The sign may be used for the verb, USE UP, or the adjective, ALL GONE.

FAMOUS

The index fingers are held in neutral space, pointing toward each other. They are brought out from the speaker's face in one or two large arcs or making several small circles as they proceed. Unlike SUCCEED, SUCCESS, the wrists do not twist so as to turn the fingers to point upward.

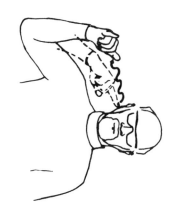

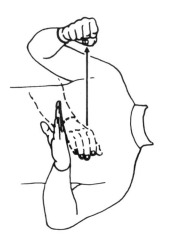
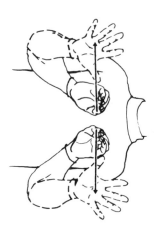

BOTH 395

The nondominant hand is held in neutral space with the palm to the side. The dominant **2** hand, palm facing the body, is brought downward in neutral space. As the **2** hand passes between the nondominant hand and the body, the nondominant hand grasps the extended fingers and holds them. The same execution with the **3** hand yields ALL THREE OF THEM and with the **4** hand ALL FOUR OF THEM. If ALL THREE OF THEM is followed by the presentation of the numeral ONE, the sign is TRIUNE or TRINITY.

BLAME 396

The nondominant fist is held palm down in neutral space, and the dominant **A** hand, thumb up, is moved forcefully forward so as to strike the back of the nondominant fist. The sign may be executed directionally. For example, the sign can be signed toward the speaker's body for BLAME MYSELF.

FIRE FROM A JOB 397

The nondominant **BENT B** hand is held palm up with the fingers pointing upward. The dominant hand, palm up, is swung across the raised fingers, striking the back of the fingers as it passes over them. An alternative execution holds the nondominant **O** hand with the opening at the top in neutral space, and the dominant hand, palm up, swings across it as if lopping its head. The field of meaning of this sign is limited to firing someone from a job. LAY OFF scrapes the fingertips of the dominant hand off the edge of the nondominant palm. In EXPELLED from school the little finger edge of the dominant **BENT B** hand is scraped forward along the nondominant palm and off its edge.

COUNTRY, COUNTRYSIDE 398

The palm or the **Y** hand are rubbed in a circular movement on the outside of the nondominant forearm, which is held at a slightly raised angle across neutral space. The sign originally referred to the rural countryside, where gentlemen wore leather patches on their sports jackets. Now the sign is also used interchangeably with NATION (the dominant **N** hand circled in neutral space and then placed on the back of the nondominant fist or wrist) to refer to a foreign country.

LOUSY 399

The thumb of the **3** hand is touched to the nose, and the hand is brought forward and then forcefully downward, so that the index and middle fingers point forward in neutral space. A more forceful execution touches the thumb of the dominant **3** hand to the nose and then strikes the hand into the raised nondominant palm.

DIVIDE 400

Both hands are held in neutral space, palms facing but with the dominant hand above the nondominant hand with the fingers crossing each other. The hands are brought down and to the side, ending with the palms down at the sides of the body. This sign is used for the arithmetic operation of DIVISION and for DIVIDING something into two parts. For DIVIDE in the sense of SHARE, the dominant hand makes slicing movements off the fingertips of the nondominant hand, palm to the side, as both hands move horizontally across the front of the body.

AFTERNOON 401

The nondominant forearm is held horizontally in neutral space, representing the horizon. The dominant forearm is rested over it in a slanting position, indicating the relative position of the sun in the afternoon sky. The lateness of the hour can be roughly indicated by the angle of the dominant forearm. For ALL AFTERNOON the execution begins with the arm near the NOON position, and it is moved through the region of the AFTERNOON, ending with a full stop in the LATE AFTERNOON position. Other signs for times of the day, MORNING, NOON, and EVENING, also use the nondominant forearm to represent the horizon.

RESPONSIBLE, RESPONSIBILITY 402

The tips of both hands are rested on the left shoulder (right shoulder for left-handed speakers). The shoulder may sag as the sign is executed to indicate a burden. The sign may be made with the dominant hand only. The sign may be initialized with **R** hands.

YOU 403

The index finger is pointed directly toward the listener. For YOU (plural) the index finger may be moved in a horizontal arc or it may stop repeatedly to indicate a specific number of persons: YOU, YOU, YOU, etc. A point is used to refer to other personal pronouns, including both subjects and objects: HE, HIM, SHE, HER, IT, THEY, and THEM. The first person plural pronoun is an exception: WE is executed by touching the tip of the index finger (WE) or the fingertips of the **U** hand to the right and left shoulder, respectively. The plural THEY and THEM may be executed with the same alternatives as the plural YOU: a sweep in an arc or several discrete references.

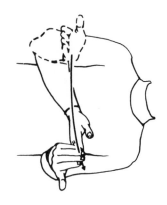

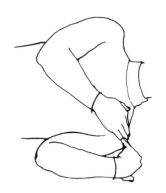

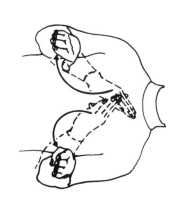

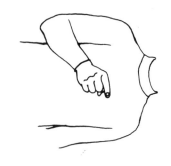

404 — FOR, PURPOSE

The tip of the index finger is touched to the forehead and then turned outward as the finger moves forward from the forehead. Originally the sign was restricted to fields of meaning involving PURPOSE, and it should probably not be used to translate *for* in the sense of *because*. Indeed, it seems to have been borrowed directly from de l'Epee, whose *Methodical Sign Language* used this sign to translate the French *pour*, providing direct evidence for a French influence on ASL, probably through the contribution of Laurent Clerc. Executed with nonverbal signals that it is a question, FOR? becomes WHAT FOR? WHY?

405 — WATER

The index finger of the **W**, palm facing left, is touched to the lips or brought near the lips one or more times. When used as a compound (WATER + SQUEEZE = WET, WATER + STREAMS = RAIN, WATER + WAVES = OCEAN), the handshape of the first element is not executed as a distinct **W**. Instead, the dominant hand merely approaches the lips or makes contact with the chin before executing the second element of the compound. The handshape of the second element of ASL compounds often spreads across both elements of the compound.

406 — FOOTBALL

The **5** hands are held with the fingers pointing upward and the palms facing in neutral space. The hands are clashed together so that the fingers intermesh with each other, representing the clashing of offensive and defensive lines of opposing football teams. Many sports are represented in ASL by imitating the action of performing the sport (SWIMMING, BOXING) or by manipulating an object used in the sport, including FISHING, POOL, ARCHERY, BASKETBALL, TENNIS, HUNTING, FENCING, *etc.*

407 — GRADUATE

The nondominant palm is held upright in neutral space, and the dominant **G** hand, index finger pointing forward, makes a small circle above the other palm and then drops down into it. The sign is generally executed as a verb. The noun, GRADUATE, would usually add the AGENT sign.

408 — LOSE

The cupped hands or the **O** hands are held in neutral space with the backs of the fingers touching. They are dropped apart so as to LOSE their contents. This sign does not translate *lose* in the sense of *lose a game*. This is signed by striking the back of the dominant **V** hand, palm up, into the upturned nondominant palm.

409 — RULE, REIGN, CONTROL

The **X** hands with the thumbs tucked against the index fingers and the palms facing each other are moved forward and backward alternately in neutral space. The sign imitates the handling of a horse's reins. The sign may be executed with **A** hands, thumbs on top and pointing forward as if holding reins.

410 — OUR

The thumb edge of the right hand is touched to the right shoulder and then the little finger edge of the right hand is touched to the left shoulder. Left handed speakers would use the left hand and touch the left and right shoulders, respectively. The open palm is the handshape used for other possessive pronouns. They are executed in the direction of their referents or toward a locus that serves as an index for their referents: MY or MINE against the chest, YOUR, YOURS toward the listener, HIS, HER, HERS, and ITS toward the noun or its index, YOUR, YOURS (plural) in a sweep or with discrete motions toward a plural number of referents, including the listener, and THEIR, THEIRS with a sweep or with discrete motions toward a plural number of referents.

411 — DISAPPEAR, DROP OUT

The raised index finger is tucked between the index and middle fingers of the nondominant hand, palm down, in neutral space, and it is pulled quickly downward so as to DROP OUT of sight. The opposite execution is POP UP, APPEAR. If the dominant index **finger** is tucked between the index and middle fingers of the nondominant hand and then brought forcefully forward and out from the body, the sign is RUN AWAY, ESCAPE, FLEE.

412 — WAY, STREET

The two hands, palms facing and fingers pointing generally downward, trace a path in neutral space as they move forward from the body. A winding movement implies a winding path, whereas a straight movement from the body implies a straight road or street. A compound, WATER + PATH = STREAM, although the handshape of the first element of the compound is likely to be an open palm rather than the marked **W** handshape.

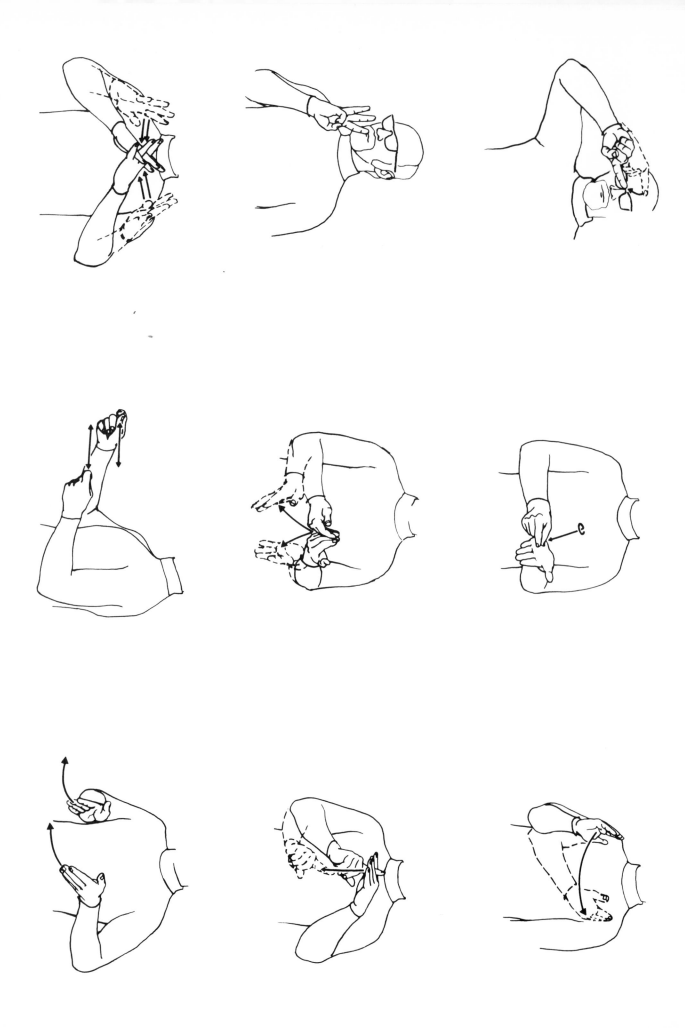

413 LOOK

The dominant V hand is held with the fingertips near the eyes, and the hand is turned with a twist of the wrist so that the fingers point forward. There are many variations in the execution of this sign using one or both hands. Turned toward the speaker, the sign is LOOK AT ME. Directed at a number of loci, the sign is LOOK AROUND. Directed over the right shoulder the sign is LOOK BACK. Executed under the nondominant hand, palm down, at eye level the sign is PROPHESY, PREDICT. Executed with both hands and a prolonged execution, the sign is WATCH. Executed with a prolonged execution and an appropriate facial expression the sign is STARE.

414 OBEY

Both A or O hands are held in front of the face with the dominant hand above the other and nearer the forehead. Both hands are brought forward and down from the face as they open into 5 hands, palms up. They body may bow slightly as the sign is executed.

415 SUBTRACT

The nondominant hand is held in neutral space with the palm to the side and the fingers pointing forward. The fingertips of the dominant C hand scrape downward on the other palm, ending in the closed A handshape. The sign represents removing something from the nondominant palm with the other hand.

416 TASTE

The middle fingertip of the OPEN 8 hand is stroked downward on the lips or toward the tongue one or more times. If the middle fingertip is touched to the chin, the sign is FAVORITE, PREFER. Touched to the chin and then brought forward from the chin with a flourish, the sign is DELICIOUS.

417 CENT

The tip of the index finger is touched to the forehead and then turned outward and up from the head, presenting the numeral 1. TWO CENTS, THREE CENTS, FOUR CENTS, FIVE CENTS, SIX CENTS, etc. are signed the same way: the index fingertip is touched to the forehead, and then the appropriate numeral is presented. The handshape of the numeral may spread across the first element of the sign, but it is still the tip of the index finger that makes contact with the forehead. Similar executions are used for a DIME (CENT + TEN), QUARTER (CENT + TWENTY FIVE), and FIFTY CENTS (CENT + FIFTY).

418 FINGERSPELL, FINGERSPELLING

The dominant 5 hand is held, palm down, in neutral space, and the fingers are wiggled. The hand may move from left to right as the sign is executed, or several brief left to right movements may be made. Fingerspelling is used in ASL primarily for proper names, technical terms, and fingerspelled signs, although it may also be used occasionally as a rhetorical device for emphasis.

419 PLAY, DRAMA

The thumbs of the A hands are held upright, and they alternately circle toward the speaker in a vertical plane, brushing against the upper chest near the shoulders. DRAMA + AGENT = ACTOR. This sign is restricted to the theater. It does not translate play in the sense of play games.

420 SECRET

The thumb nail of the dominant A hand is pressed against the lips or tapped repeatedly on the chin. Followed by a movement under the palm of the nondominant hand, the sign is HIDE.

421 GROUP

The cupped hands, palms facing outward, complete a circle as they are brought together in neutral space so as to enclose a GROUP. In the final position, the palms face the speaker. This sign may be initialized with G for GROUP, C for CLASS, F for FAMILY, and T for TEAM. Any noun modified by the sign GROUP is automatically pluralized: SOLDIER + GROUP = ARMY, COW + GROUP = HERD, etc.

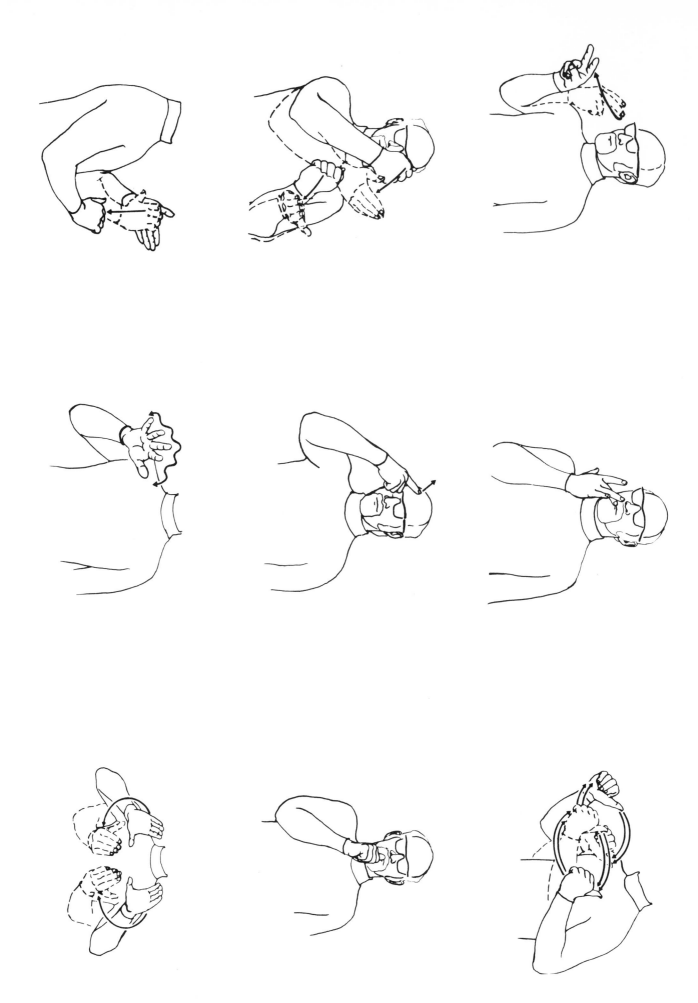

HOUR

The fingers of the closed hand with the index finger pointing upward are placed against the nondominant palm, which faces to the side with the fingers pointing upward. The dominant hand makes a full circle on the other palm, either with the index finger pointing upward the whole time or with the index finger making a circle like the hour hand of a clock as the wrist twists appropriately. Executed with a numeral on the dominant hand, the sign is TWO HOURS, THREE HOURS, *etc.* Executed with the T hand, the sign is the generic TIME.

WEDDING

The nondominant hand is held with the fingers pointing downward and the palm toward the body. The dominant hand is held similarly some distance away. Both hands are brought toward each other in upward arcs, and the dominant hand grasps the fingertips of the nondominant hand, imitating the formal joining of hands in wedlock. The verb, MARRY, is executed by clasping the C hands together in neutral space.

SECOND, MINUTE

The fingers of the closed hand with the index finger pointing upward are placed against the nondominant palm, which faces to the side with the fingers pointing upward. The dominant hand is twisted at the wrist so that the index finger moves forward past the fingertips of the other palm The length of the movement can imply a longer or shorter duration, as in MINUTE or SECOND.

RED

The tip of the index finger is brushed downward on the lips or chin one or more times. Executed with the P hand, the sign is PINK. Followed by the 5 hands, palms toward the face, moving up the face alternately or simultaneously, the sign is BLUSH, EMBARRASSED. Followed by the thumbs and index fingers of both hands forming a circle around the face, the sign is RED FACED, or EMBARRASSED.

DIFFICULT, HARD

The knuckles of the two BENT V hands are struck together in front of the body as they pass each other going up and down in opposite directions (alternating movement). The action may be repeated several times. If the middle finger knuckle of the BENT V hand is struck against the back of the nondominant fist, the sign is HARD. If the index finger knuckle of the BENT V hand is struck against the bridge of the nose, the sign is STRICT. If the knuckles of both BENT V hands are jammed against each other several times as the wrists are twisted alternately in opposite directions, the sign is PROBLEM.

SIGN YOUR NAME, REGISTER

The fingertips of the extended middle and index fingers are slapped into the edge of the nondominant palm. If the sign is reduplicated as the hands move down in space, the sign is FILL OUT FORMS, SIGN FORMS. Since a signature on a form is often needed for a job application, the sign may also refer to APPLY FOR A JOB.

EASY

The nondominant hand is held, palm up, in neutral space, and the fingertips of the dominant hand, palm up, are brushed lightly against the back of the other fingers two or more times. The facial expression often displays confidence.

TEMPT, TEMPTATION

The nondominant forearm is held across the chest, and the tip of the bent index finger of the dominant hand is tapped on the nondominant elbow two or more times. The *underhandedness* of the temptation is implied by the position of the dominant hand under the other arm as the sign is executed.

STOP

The nondominant hand is held, palm up, in neutral space, and the dominant hand, palm to the left and fingers pointing forward, is brought down so as to strike the little finger edge of the hand in the nondominant palm. The sign can serve as an imperative, *Stop that!*

 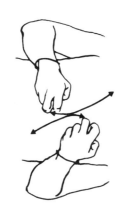 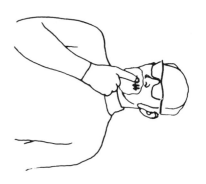

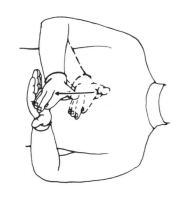 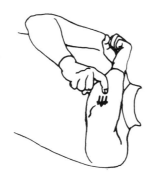 

EMPHASIZE, IMPRESS

The nondominant hand is held, palm up, in neutral space. The thumb of the dominant hand is pressed into the nondominant palm and twisted forcefully. The sign may be used as a one-word sentence, meaning *I am impressed.*

US

The fingertips of the raised middle and index fingers of the right hand are touched to the right and then the left shoulder. Alternatively, the fingers may point downward as the sign is executed. Left handed speakers would executed the sign with the left hand, touching the left and then the right shoulder. The same sign executed with the index finger is WE.

AROUND

The fingertips and thumb of the nondominant hand are clustered together in the **BABY O** handshape with the fingers pointing up. The index finger of the dominant hand circles the clustered fingertips clockwise for right handed speakers. **ABOUT** is signed similarly, but the clustered fingers of the nondominant hand point to the side instead of up.

DON'T KNOW

The fingertips of the dominant hand are placed on the forehead, as in KNOW, and the hand is then turned outward with a twist of the wrist. This negative inflection also produces BAD (the fingertips are placed near the mouth and then the hand is turned outward), DON'T WANT (the **CLAW** hands, palms up in neutral space, are turned over abruptly), and DON'T LIKE (the **F** hand, palm toward the chest, is flicked away with a twist of the wrist). For emphasis, DON'T KNOW may be executed with two hands.

WAIT

The hands are held, palms up, off to the side of the body, with the nondominant hand somewhat farther from the body than the dominant hand. The fingers are bent several times from the open hands into the **BENT B** handshape, or the fingers are wiggled.

PRAY, ASK

The palms of both hands are pressed together in front of the body in the traditional prayerful posture, fingers pointing upward. If the praying hands make an arc toward the speaker's body, the sign is the verb, ASK, MAKE A REQUEST. An alternative sign ASK traces a question mark in the air in the direction of the person to whom the question is addressed. This latter sign may be executed toward the speaker as a reflexive, *I ask myself.*

WINE

The **W** hand is circled at the right cheek with the palm toward the cheek. The same sign with the **V** hand is VINEGAR.

DARK

The two hands, palms toward the face and fingers pointing upward, are moved across the face so that the wrists are crossed. The sign implies obscured vision, and the eyes may squint as the sign is executed. A related sign, VAGUE, presents both **5** hands, palms facing, in front of the face and circles them alternately counterclockwise as the eyes are squinted as if trying to see through the moving fingers.

GRAVY

The nondominant hand is held with the palm to the side, fingers pointing forward. The thumb and index finger of the dominant hand grasp the underside of the nondominant hand and slide off. The action is repeated two or more times. A related sign, MEAT, grasps the fleshy part of the nondominant hand between the thumb and index finger with the thumb and index finger of the dominant hand.

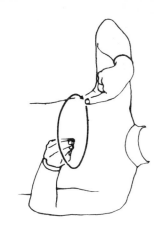  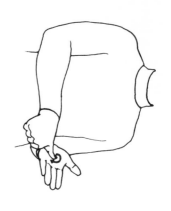

 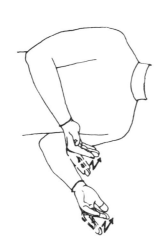 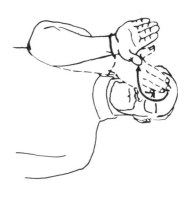

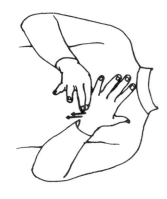 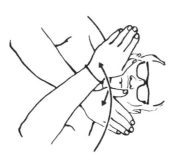 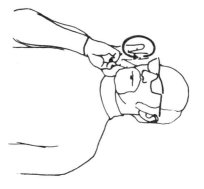

440 FALSE, LIE

The BENT B hand is brushed across the mouth or lips. The movement is right to left for right handed speakers. An alternative execution uses the horizontal extended index finger instead of the BENT B hand. Both BENT B hands may be used, the one above the other, moving in opposite directions across the mouth and chin.

441 SUMMER, HOT

The X hand is held in a horizontal plane with the tip of the index finger pointing downward. It is drawn across the forehead from left to right in the case of right handed speakers. The sign imitates the act of wiping perspiration from the brow.

442 FEEL

The tip of the middle finger of the OPEN 8 hand is stroked on the chest over the heart. If this is followed by a second movement extended out from the body toward an imaginary object of the verb, the sign is PITY. If FEEL is followed by a quick twist of the wrist, turning the hand away from the body, the sign is TOUCHY, SENSITIVE.

443 SMART, CLEVER, INTELLIGENT

The middle finger of the OPEN 8 handshape is touched to the forehead, and the hand is then turned quickly outward and upward with a twist of the wrist. The sign typically refers to someone who is quick and clever. The more enduring trait, WISE, is executed by moving the tip of the curved index finger, with the tip pointing downward, down along the forehead one or more times. The sign WISE may be motivated by the notion of plumbing the depths of the mind.

444 FINE, POLITE, FANCY

The thumb of the 5 hand is placed against the chest as the fingers are wiggled. An alternative execution taps the thumb of the 5 hand against the chest two or more times. A third alternative touches the thumb of the 5 hand to the chest and then brings the hand upward and outward with a flamboyant flourish. This is the common answer to the question, *How are you?* It also can be used for the adjective FANCY or POLITE. For example, FINE ROOM is a permissible translation for *living room*.

445 GET, OBTAIN, RECEIVE

The 5 hands are held extended in front of the body, and they are brought toward the body as they close into fists, the one resting on top of the other. Signed forcefully with just one hand the sign is TAKE.

446 LIVE, LIFE

The A or L hands, palms toward the body, are drawn upward against the front of the body. WHAT YOUR LIVE? is translated, *What is your address?*

447 MONEY

The back of the dominant BABY O hand is tapped into the nondominant palm in neutral space. Thrown out from the palm as the fingers are spread into the 5 hand, the sign is WASTE. Moved forward from the palm in a small arc, the sign is BUY. A reduplicated BUY with the hands moving in a horizontal arc is SHOP, SHOPPING. MONEY is used in two compounds. MONEY + WOW! (the 5 hand shaken vigorously at the waist) is EXPENSIVE. MONEY + MUCH = RICH (for MUCH the cupped hands are held in neutral space, the dominant hand above the nondominant hand with the palms facing, and the dominant hand is moved upward so as to imply a pile of money).

448 WANT

The CLAW hands, palms up, are drawn toward the body. If both claw hands are curled inward forcefully several times, the sign is GRASPING, GREEDY. WANT may be inflected with an incorporated negative by turning oth hands over with a twist of the wrists. A stronger sign for WANT, WISH, LONG FOR draws the thumb and fingers of the C hand down the upper chest.

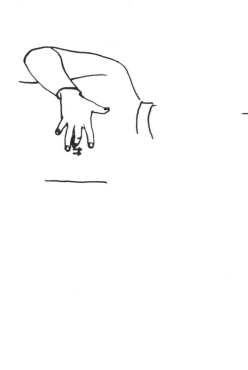

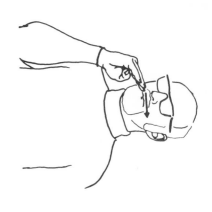

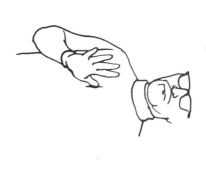

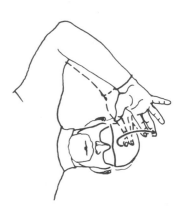

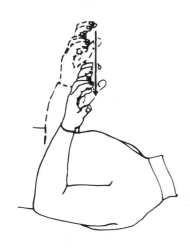

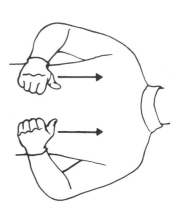

AWKWARD 449

The nondominant hand is held, palm up, in neutral space, and the dominant M hand makes a small circle and then touches the middle of the other palm. This sign may be used for DOWNTOWN.

MIDDLE, CENTER 450

The extended dominant index finger, pointing forward, is thrust under the nondominant hand, palm down, in neutral space. The sign may be executed with the dominant K hand. KILL + AGENT = KILLER.

KILL 451

The nondominant 5 hand is held in neutral space with the palm toward the speaker's body. The extended index finger of the dominant hand weaves a path downward AMONG the extended fingers of the nondominant hand, from the index to the little finger. The extended index finger generally does not actually move between the fingers; the movement is executed near the tips of the fingers.

AMONG 452

The index fingers of both hands are pointed forward with the palms down in neutral space, and they are placed along side each other, usually a short distance between the two movements. The hands may move laterally a short distance between the two movements. This sign is used in some compounds: THINK + SAME = AGREE, MALE + SAME = BROTHER, FEMALE + SAME = SISTER. An alternative sign SAME, SIMILAR is executed with the palm down Y hand in neutral space moved laterally between the items being compared. Executed between the listener and speaker, this sign is ME TOO, I AGREE.

SAME, ALSO, TOO 453

The dominant V hand is swung across the face by bending the wrist one or more times. Both hands may be used moving in opposite directions across the face. The adverb, CARELESSLY, may be signaled nonmanually by thrusting the tongue against the back of the teeth with glazed eyes as the verb is executed which incorporates the adverb.

CARELESS, CARELESSLY 454

The dominant hand, palm down, is placed in the nondominant hand, palm up, the positions are, then, reversed, and, finally, both hands are brought down and out in neutral space, ending with the palms facing downward at the sides of the body. A related sign, QUIET, omits the first two syllables, and merely begins the sign near the lips, bringing the hands down and out to the sides of the body, palms down. This latter sign may be executed directionally and with some force as an imperative, BE QUIET.

PEACE 455

The 3 hands, palms down and fingers pointing forward, make awkward stepping motions alternately in neutral space. The sign is used not only for an awkward physical gait but also for feeling mentally ILL AT EASE or AWKWARD. A related sign, CRIPPLED, uses the two index fingers pointing downward to represent legs, and they are moved so as to make limping steps in neutral space with an uneven gait.

SUNSHINE 456

The index finger draws a small circle in the air above eye level, and then the BABY O handshape, fingers pointing downward, is brought downward in neutral space as the hand opens into the 5 hand, representing rays of SUNSHINE coming down from the sky. In an alternative version, the thumb of the C hand is touched to the forehead, and then the second element of the sign is executed. To restrict the field of meaning to SUN with no reference to its shining, the thumb of the C hand may be touched to the forehead, and then the hand is moved up and away from the forehead in an arc. MOON is signed similarly, but the thumb of the C hand is touched to the cheek bone instead of the forehead.

WIN, VICTORY 457

The nondominant fist is held in neutral space with the palm to the side. The dominant C hand is swung swiftly down and to the side so as to graze the top of the left fist as it passes. In the final position the dominant hand is a clenched fist. The action is said to imitate the grasping and raising of an Olympic torch. VICTORY may also be signed by waving imaginary flags above the head with both clenched fists. This latter sign also means ANNIVERSARY or CELEBRATE.

  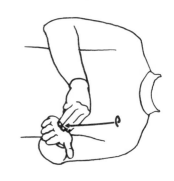

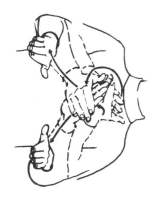  

  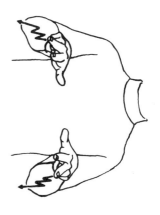

458 TOUCH

The nondominant hand or fist is held, palm down, in neutral space, and the middle finger of the dominant OPEN 8 hand is touched to the back of the other hand. If the middle finger moves outward along the back of the hand, the sign is NAKED, BARE, EMPTY. If the finger touches the hand and then the OPEN 8 hand is raised up from the fist in a waving motion, the sign is SHINY.

459 WHITE

The fingertips of the 5 hand brush the chest into the BABY O handshape as it moves forward from the body. The sign may be motivated by the notion of touching something white, namely, a white shirt. If the sign WHITE is followed by a sign which opens the BABY O handshape into a 5 hand, palm toward the face, the sign is PALE FACED, WHITE FACED, or the racial designation, WHITE.

460 DEAF, ACOUSTICALLY DEAF

The index finger points to the ear, and then both hands, palms facing out and fingers pointing up are brought together at the midline as in the sign CLOSE, CLOSED. This is the sign for ACOUSTICALLY DEAF. The sign for DEAF that refers to members of the deaf community, those who are CULTURALLY DEAF, touches the index finger to the mouth and cheek or to the cheek and mouth. HARD OF HEARING is a fingerspelled abbreviation, H-H in neutral space.

461 COUNT

The nondominant palm is held palm to the side and fingers pointing forward or upward in neutral space. The tip of the thumb and index finger of the dominant F hand touch the left palm repeatedly as the F hand moves up the other palm toward the fingertips in a series of small arcs. An alternative execution moves the F hand up the nondominant palm in a single, smooth movement.

462 CLEAR, BRIGHT, LIGHT

The two O hands are held in neutral space with the thumb tips touching or very close together. They are brought up and to the side as they open into 5 hands, palms facing outward. A light that casts a beam is generally represented by a change from the BABY O to the 5 handshape as the hand moves in a straight line in the direction that the beam is expected to shine. For example, both hands aimed forward from the body can represent HEADLIGHTS, and the nondominant fist can serve as the locus for a beam that represents a FLASHLIGHT. If the hand is opened repeatedly from the BABY O to the 5 handshape, this represents a blinking light. If the 5 handshape is swung around in a circle one or more times, the sign refers to the light on a police car or ambulance.

463 GALLAUDET, GALLAUDET UNIVERSITY

The dominant G hand is brought out from the side of the head at the eye as the thumb and index finger come into contact. The sign is motivated by the act of grasping and removing a pair of glasses. Thomas Hopkins Gallaudet wore such glasses, and this was his name sign. It later became the sign for GALLAUDET COLLEGE, which is now GALLAUDET UNIVERSITY. Usually the sign COLLEGE or UNIVERSITY is used in addition to the sign GALLAUDET to refer to the institution. COLLEGE claps both hands together and then raises the dominant hand above the other in a spiral. For UNIVERSITY, the dominant hand changes into a U handshape as the sign is executed.

464 PAPER

The dominant hand, palm down, is brushed two or more times along the heel of the nondominant hand, palm up, as the dominant hand moves across it toward the heel. The sign is said to represent paper fed through a printing press.

465 SPEECHREAD, SPEECH

The BENT V hand, fingertips toward the mouth, makes a small oval around the mouth one or more times. This sign refers to the act of speechreading or to speech classes in school. LIPREAD is executed with the V hand, fingertips pointing toward the mouth, moved back and forth across the mouth two or more times.

466 HATE, DESPISE

The curved middle fingers of both hands are held tightly by the thumbs (the 8 handshape), and they are flicked out once forcefully from the body or several times in quick succession. An alternative sign turns the palm out away from the body and thrusts the palm away from the body as if to DESPISE or SHUN someone or something. The head may be turned aside as these signs are executed. The facial expression is likely to display hostility.

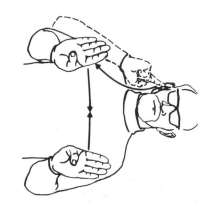
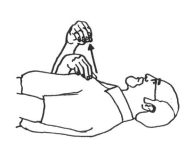
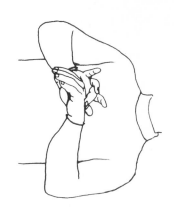

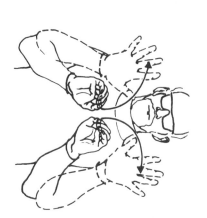
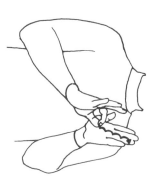
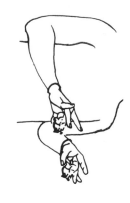
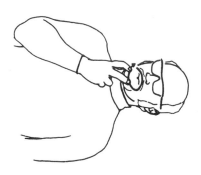
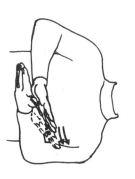

FREE, SAVE 467

The wrists are crossed as in the sign, BOUND, with the fists clenched and the palms down. The hands are pulled forcefully apart with a twist of both wrists, leaving the arms FREE. SAVE + AGENT = SAVIOR. The sign FREE may be executed with F hands.

CONSCIENCE, GUILT 468

The right extended index finger, palm down, is struck horizontally over the heart two times. Related signs include CHARACTER (the C hand rubbed in a circle over the heart), PERSONALITY (the P hand circled near the heart and then placed over it), and RELIGION (the horizontal R hand placed above the heart and brought forward from the chest in a slight upward arc).

YOUR 469

The open palm, fingers pointing up, is directed toward the listener For the plural form, the open palm is directed either in an arc or to several discrete loci, which include the listener. The open palm is used for all of the possessive pronouns in ASL. MY is executed against the chest. HIS, HER, HERS, ITS is executed in the direction of the person or thing to which the pronoun refers or in the direction of a locus established as an index for the antecedents to these pronouns. THEIR is executed as a sweep or as discrete references to loci which do not include the listener. OUR is a minor exception: the index finger edge of the right palm is touched to the right shoulder, and the hand is moved in an arc so that the little finger edge of the palm touches the left shoulder. Left-handed speakers would do the opposite.

FINISH, END 470

The nondominant arm is held horizontally in neutral space with the palm to the side and fingers pointing forward. The dominant hand, palm down, is moved forward over the nondominant arm and hand until it reaches the fingertips, and then it makes a 90 degree angle, turning downward with the palm to the side, as it moves down in front of the fingertips. The sign is not typically used as a temporal adverb. It is a verb, FINISH, COMPLETE, an adjective, DONE, COMPLETED, or a noun, END, COMPLETION.

ONCE 471

The nondominant hand is held, palm up, in neutral space, and the extended dominant index fingertip is struck in the palm and raised up to present the numeral, ONE. A similar execution with the numerals TWO and THREE results in TWICE and THREE TIMES. If the sign ONCE is reduplicated, ONCE, ONCE, ONCE, the sign is SOMETIMES. If the reduplication is very slow, the sign is RARELY, ONCE IN A GREAT WHILE.

IMPROVE 472

The nondominant arm is held horizontally in neutral space, and the dominant hand, palm to the side, makes small, stepwise movements up the nondominant arm toward the inside of the elbow, touching the arm with the little finger edge of the dominant hand repeatedly as it moves up the arm. A dramatic improvement may be implied by a single sizable movement in an arc from the wrist to a point near the inside of the elbow of the nondominant arm. The opposite movement, with the dominant hand going down the nondominant forearm in small arcs toward the wrist, is DETERIORATE.

BIG, WIDE 473

Both hands are held in neutral space with the palms facing and they are brought apart to a full stop. The opposite action is SMALL, NARROW. For BIG, LARGE, the sign is generally executed with L hands, with the index finger slightly curled as the sign is executed. For emphasis the hands may be elevated as they are drawn apart and then come down again in an abrupt movement to a full stop. For MUCH CLAW hands are used, and for VERY V hands are used. Relative size in ASL is always tied to some extent to the real world and its appearances. The sign BIG above does not translate *a big tree* or *a big bug*. The signs SMALL, SHORT, and TINY would be executed according to the same principle.

GIVE, DONATE 474

The fingers of both hands are held together as if they have something between them, and they are moved forward in an arc toward the real or imagined recipient. The sign may be executed with one hand. This is a directional verb, executed toward the indirect object. GIVE ME is executed toward the speaker's body, and EXCHANGE GIFTS is executed by presenting the two hands in opposite directions in neutral space, ending with the wrists crossed. The sign may be executed with one or both X hands, with the arc made by bending the wrists as the palms face each other. The sign may be modified to accommodate the size and shape of the object of the verb.

DISAPPOINT, DISAPPOINTED 475

The index finger of the dominant hand is pointed toward the speaker's face, and it is jabbed toward the chin. The head is likely to be bowed slightly as the sign is executed, and the facial expression will register disappointment. A related sign, BITTER, pinches the lips together and squints the eyes as the index finger is jabbed toward the mouth.

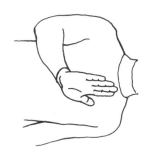  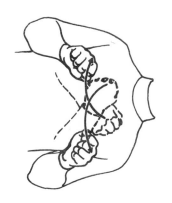

 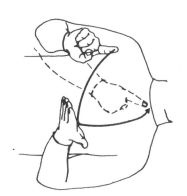 

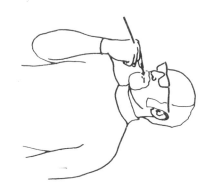  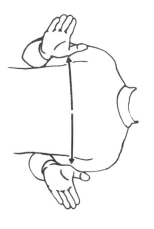

WITH

Both fists, thumbs up, are held next to each other in neutral space so that the knuckles of both hands are in contact. If the hands move forward in neutral space, the sign is ACCOM-PANY, GO WITH. If the hands are dropped apart into 5 hands, palms down, the sign is WITHOUT.

CHEESE

The palms of both hands are pressed together in a horizontal plane in neutral space, and the wrists are twisted so that the hands move in opposite directions as the palms are squeezed against each other. The sign may be motivated by the action associated with squeezing out the liquid by-products from the curds of cheese. The movement may be repeated back and forth.

BABY

The back of the dominant hand, representing the baby's head, is rested in the nondominant palm in neutral space, and the hands are gently moved up and down. An alternative execution lays the back of the dominant hand along the horizontal nondominant forearm, and the arms are rocked. MALE + BABY = SON, FEMALE + BABY = DAUGHTER. In the compounds, the movement in the second element is dropped, and the handshape may remain the same (the open hand) throughout the execution.

AVENGE, REVENGE

The tips of the pinched thumbs and index fingertips are struck against each other in neutral space. A related sign, PICK ON, uses the same handshape on the dominant hand, and it is struck against the raised index finger of the nondominant hand, which represents the object of the verb.

PROUD, PRIDE

The thumb of the dominant A hand is toward the chest so that the thumb nail is toward the chest, and the thumb is drawn up the chest. The chest may be puffed out as the sign is executed. If the thumb of the A hand is punched against the side of the chest repeatedly, the sign is BOAST, BRAG.

DISAPPEAR, MELT, DISSOLVE

The 5 hands are held in neutral space, palms toward the speaker's face or palms facing, and they are drawn apart as they move downward in an arc and close into fists, palms facing each other. The sign may be executed slowly to represent a gradual disappearance or dissolving. An alternative sign, DISAPPEAR, DROP OUT OF SIGHT, tucks the raised index finger of the dominant hand between the middle and index finger of the nondominant hand, palm down, and then pulls it down and OUT OF SIGHT with a quick movement.

MONTH

The nondominant index finger is held upright in neutral space, palm and the horizontal index finger of the dominant hand, palm toward the speaker's body, is stroked down the side of the raised, nondominant index finger. Number can be incorporated in the execution by presenting the appropriate numeral on the dominant hand as the sign is executed. For example, TWO MONTHS is executed with the TWO hand, and the contact with the nondominant index finger is made by the middle finger of the dominant hand. The sign, MONTH, can be redu-plicated for EVERY MONTH, MONTHLY.

FOX

The circle formed by the thumb and index finger of the dom-inant F hand is placed over the tip of the nose with the other fingers pointing upward, and the hand is rocked back and forth by bending the wrist repeatedly. WOLF is also executed at the nose: the 5 hand is held with the palm toward the face at the nose, and it moves forward from the face as the fingers close into the BABY O handshape. The fingers trace the outline of the wolf's snout.

CHANGE

The X hands are held in neutral space in opposed positions, palms facing, with one hand above the other. The hands exchange places with a twist of both wrists, so that the palms are still facing each other, but the other hand is on top. An alternative execution holds the X hands in neutral space with the palms facing and neither hand above the other. They move across the midline so that in the final position the wrists are crossed.

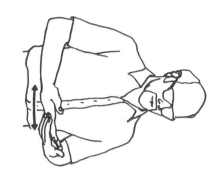 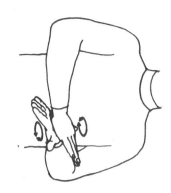 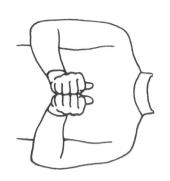

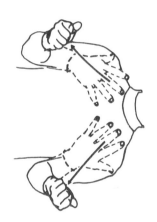 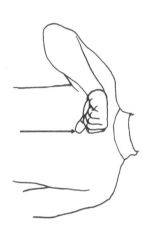 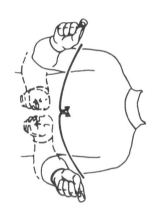

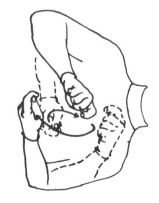  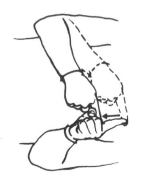

485 AMERICA

The fingers of both **5** hands are interlocked in neutral space, and the hands are moved in a horizontal, counterclockwise circle. The sign is said to be motivated by logs, as in a log cabin or split rail fence, or by the concept of a melting pot. The UNITED STATES is also represented by means of the fingerspelled sign, U.S.

486 SUCCEED, SUCCESS

The index fingers are held at the sides of the face pointing upward with the palms toward the face. They are turned out and up with a twist of both wrists sometimes with a double motion and a small circle in the middle of the execution. The sign is used for a wide variety of gratifying experiences, from winning a game to getting a job to finding the used car one was looking for. It is often executed as a one-word sentence.

487 CONFESS, CONFESSION

The fingertips of both **BENT B** hands brush up against the body toward the heart, and then the hands are brought up and out, ending with the open hands, palms up, in neutral space. The sign implies opening the heart and revealing what is there. The CONFESSIONAL used in Roman Catholic Church is signed by crossing the fingers of both **5** hands at the sides of the head with the palms toward the face side of the head. The sign represents the screened lattice that protects the privacy of the person making confession.

488 MAGIC

The fists are held side by side, palms down, in neutral space, and they are opened quickly into F hands, palms down, as the hands move forward from the body. The sign imitates the action of a magician who is directing his hands at a device that is used in the act.

489 HOME

The tips of the clustered fingers of the **BABY O** handshape are touched near the lips and on the cheek. If the previous sign left the dominant hand off to the side of the head, the contact may be reversed to touch first the cheek and then a location on or near the lips. The sign may be motivated by the notion that HOME is where you eat and sleep.

490 DEVIL

The thumb of the **3** hand is touched to the side of the head, and the extended index and middle fingers are curled inward two or more times. Both hands may be used. The sign may represent the Biblical SATAN or a mischievous person. ANGEL is signed by touching both hands to the shoulders and then either waving the arms as wings or tracing the outline of wings.

491 EAT

The clustered fingertips of the **BABY O** handshape are brought to the mouth. For the noun, FOOD, the sign is repeated in a tensed execution. The verb, EAT, is a single, smooth movement toward the mouth. If both hands are used alternately, the sign is FEAST, BANQUET. If the **BENT B** hand moves past the mouth and over the shoulder, the sign IS CONSUME, EAT IT ALL UP. The compound, FOOD (without the repeated movement) + GIVE (two handed) is the transitive verb, FEED.

492 BAD

The fingertips of the dominant hand are brought near the mouth, palm toward the mouth, as in GOOD. The palm is then turned forcibly away from the face as the hand moves away from the face. The facial expression is likely to be disagreeable. The opposite, GOOD, brings the fingertips of the hand toward the mouth with the palm facing the mouth, and the hand is then dropped downward, generally in the upturned palm of the nondominant hand.

493 EXCITED

The middle fingers of both hands in the **OPEN 8** handshape alternately brush against the upper chest as they move alternately upward along the chest. If the sign is executed with a simultaneous instead of an alternating movement, the sign is THRILLED or the idiom, WHAT'S HAPPENING? If the tips of the middle fingers of the **OPEN 8** hands are touched against the chest and then the hands are allowed to droop or sag downward, the sign is DEPRESSED.

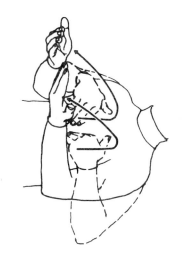 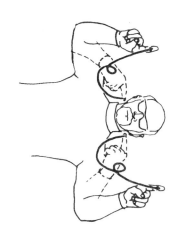 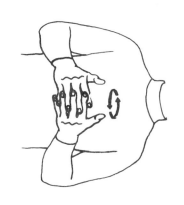

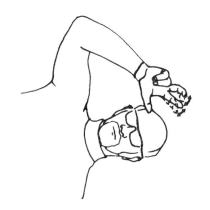 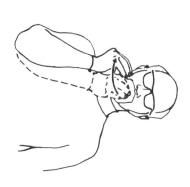 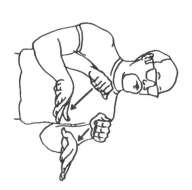

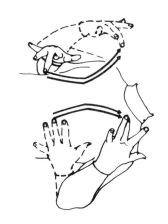 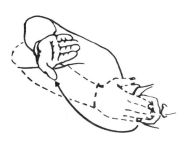 

494 ALL

The nondominant hand is held, palm up, in neutral space, and the dominant hand, palm down, makes a sweeping movement in a horizontal, clockwise circle, ending palm up in the palm of the nondominant hand. The sign implies gathering everything within reach and holding it in both hands.

495 HELP

The fingertips of the dominant hand, palm up, are placed under the nondominant fist, palm to the side, and gently raise the fist in neutral space. If the dominant hand is initialized with the **A** hand, and the raised thumb gently touches the bottom of the nondominant fist, the sign is ASSIST. Followed by the AGENT sign, it is ASSISTANT. If the flat surface formed by the fingers of the dominant fist push up from under the nondominant fist in neutral space, the sign is SUPPORT. Reduplicated as the hands move laterally in space, the sign is FOUNDATION.

496 FEW

The dominant **A** hand is held in neutral space, palm up, and the fingers are slowly peeled out, one at a time, beginning with the index finger. The final position is the **4** hand, palm up, in neutral space. If both hands are used and the movement is not slowed, the sign is SEVERAL. If both fists are unfurled so that all the fingers are extended at once, palms up, the sign is MANY. The movement may be repeated for MANY.

497 NEXT YEAR

The nondominant fist is held in neutral space, palm to the right. The dominant fist, index finger extended, is touched to the top of the nondominant fist, and it then is moved forward and slightly upward in an arc. If the sign is executed with the **2** or **3** hand, respectively, the sign is TWO YEARS FROM NOW or THREE YEARS FROM NOW. If the movement is back over the shoulder, the sign is LAST YEAR, TWO YEARS AGO, THREE YEARS AGO. A similar inflection for number and tense can be applied to the sign WEEK. NEXT YEAR reduplicated with the index finger uncurled with each forward movement is EVERY YEAR, ANNUALLY.

498 HOT

The palm of the **CLAW** hand is faced toward the open mouth, and the hand is turned out and away from the mouth abruptly. An alternative sign wipes the brow with a horizontal movement of the **X** hand. HOT TO THE TOUCH is represented by signing TOUCH (the middle finger of the **OPEN 8** handshape is touched to the back of the nondominant fist), and the hand is then shaken as if it has just touched something hot. A related sign, WARM, places the fist near the mouth with the palm toward the mouth, and the fingers are gently unfurled into the **5** handshape, with the palm still toward the mouth, as if feeling the warmth of the breath.

499 WORLD

The dominant **W** hand is placed on the nondominant **W** hand or on the top of the nondominant fist. The dominant hand then makes a full circle around the nondominant fist or **W** handshape, ending in the original position. The sign is related to YEAR, which circles the nondominant fist with the dominant fist, representing one revolution of the earth around the sun.

500 FEMALE

The thumb of the dominant **A** hand is brushed along the jaw. The sign is derived from bonnet strings. It is used in several compounds: FEMALE + SHORT = GIRL, FEMALE + MARRY = WIFE, FEMALE + SAME = SISTER, FEMALE + FINE = LADY, FEMALE + BABY = DAUGHTER, FEMALE + TALL = WOMAN. The handshape of the second element of these compounds may spread across both syllables.

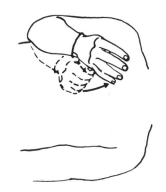 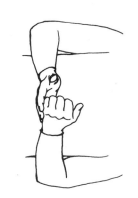 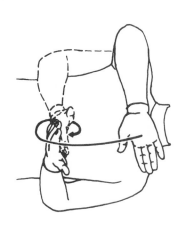

 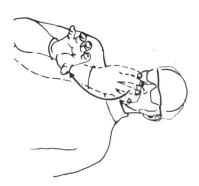